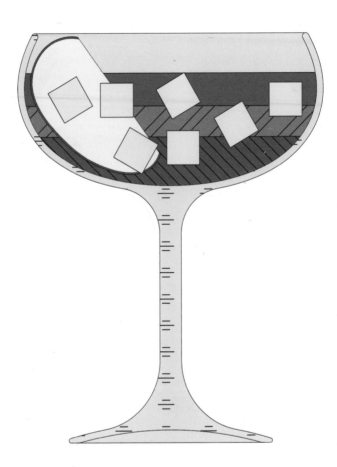

WHISKY

Shake, Muddle, Stir

Whisky: Shake, Muddle, Stir by Dan Jones

First published in 2023 by Hardie Grant Books,
an imprint of Hardie Grant Publishing

Hardie Grant Books (UK)
52–54 Southwark Street
London SE1 1UN

Hardie Grant Books (Australia)
Ground Floor, Building 1
658 Church Street
Melbourne, VIC 3121

hardiegrantbooks.com

British Library Cataloguing-in-Publication Data. A catalogue record
for this book is available from the British Library.

ISBN: 978-1-78488-656-1
10 9 8 7 6 5 4 3 2 1

Publishing Director: Kajal Mistry
Senior Editor: Eila Purvis
Art Direction: Matt Phare
Illustrator: Daniel Servansky
Copy-editor: Meredith Olson
Proofreader: Kathy Steer
Indexer: Cathy Heath

Colour Reproduction by p2d
Printed and bound in China by Leo Paper Group

WHISKY

Shake, Muddle, Stir

by Dan Jones

ILLUSTRATIONS BY DANIEL SERVANSKY

Hardie Grant

BOOKS

CONTENTS

Welcome
to
WHISKY
Shake, Muddle, Stir

FIRE, SMOKE AND LOVE

We are not born whisky lovers. Most of us must steal our first teenage sip from a grandparents' liquor cabinet, or a carelessly tipsy relative at a wedding, and it's all fire and smoke and instant regret. We'll gasp, our eyes stinging, and wonder what all the fuss is about. But whisky will haunt you, bringing you back to it again and again, until your affection for it knows no bounds. Perhaps it's this harsh but memorable meet-cute that makes whisky lodge in our minds, giving it a permanent home in our top 10 most beloved bar orders. And it's also the drink we turn to for gifts for loved ones, and special moments of personal celebration.

This book has a collection of over 40 of the very best whisky cocktails, from tried and tested classics sipped by the stars of old to fresh new ideas of how to love and load your favourite whiskies, ryes and bourbons; they are easy and inspiring recipes to make at home. Not a whisky or bourbon lover just yet? If you need a little convincing, create the perfect Old Fashioned using a cut-crystal glass, an orange-peel twist large enough to whack your nose and a huge cube of perfectly clear ice. Then dim the lights, put on your favourite track and sip and kick back. You'll fall in love in no time.

Dan Jones

Back In The habit: Let's Raise A Glass To The Whisky Monks

'Too much of anything is bad, but too much good whiskey is barely enough.' – Mark Twain

Over the centuries, whisky has been iconised as the world's most beloved spirit, but it wasn't always a pathway to pleasure. It was once a lifesaver in medieval medicine and, originally made in monasteries, was the warm breath up a monk's draughty robes. The dark, grain spirit has been distilled illicitly in basements in Prohibition-era USA, traded, bartered and fought over, and poured for kings, queens and the delightfully degenerate in equal measure. Whisky has also been reimagined, poked at and teased, and is now a spectrum of taste and type that is sipped and slammed back by drinkers across the world. Today, glittering on the backbar, it lives on in all its amber iterations: from classic whisky and international premium blends to smooth and sweet bourbon, peppery rye and eye-popping moonshine. Its woody, caramel and sometimes smoky, fiery taste is completely its own – and otherworldly.

Let's take the *Outlander Express* back to the ancient isles of Scotland and a delicious concoction known as usquebaugh, a Gaelic term that means 'water of life' and was used to describe all manner of ancient alcoholic pick-me-ups. Monks delivered the science of distillation to Scotland and Ireland sometime between 1100 and 1300, hitching up their cassocks and setting to work. But it was their dogged and divine transformation of simple barley beer that supercharged it into a whisky-like spirit. Eventually, these distilled spirits were considered a medicine, and whisky was rare and revered, but by the late 15th century it evolved again and was made and imbibed for intense pleasure. In a way, whisky has changed very little in the last 500 years, and alongside its bright, complex cousins, is now the world's most popular and well-known spirit.

Although whisky has its spiritual and ancient home in Scotland (hence its nickname, Scotch), whiskey – with an e – is considered an Irish and, latterly, North American, concoction. Just to confuse matters, there are more than 80 other nations that also make the spirit and almost all spell it 'whisky', too. Plus, the US has its own version from Kentucky, known as bourbon (where the mash is 51 per cent corn, aged in freshly charred white oak barrels, bottled between 80 and 160 proof, and is known for being a little sweeter). Alongside bourbon, some might say moonshine – homemade and high-proof – is the unofficial booze of the US state, with its history of Prohibition, dry counties and creative bootleggers who set about to make their own whiskey. The Canadians and Japanese are also major makers of the amber spirit, and India is the biggest drinker of it.

Single grain Scotch whisky – always made in a single distillery – is created from a single crop of grain, malted or unmalted, and water, and single malt Scotch whisky is its exotic, rare cousin that also derives from a single distillery and uses malted mash (Japanese versions of this are delicious). The major Scottish producers are still in places like Islay and the Highlands, their antique equipment and secret processes adding complex flavours and aromas. Blended

Scotch whisky is the delicious fusion of grain and malt Scotch, and cask strength Scotch is siphoned directly from the cask to the bottle, cutting out the middleman, for a purer (but perhaps less interesting) taste. And those expensive aged Scotches seem to reach maturity and the height of their popularity at around 18 years old.

Those investments distillers made decades ago are now looking rosy: the contemporary whisky world is growing. We're drinking more of it and making more of it, too. In terms of growth, it's the softer, more accessible Irish whiskey that's leading the charge and, alongside American bourbon, is finding a new home with young first timers, before they graduate onto classic whisky or Scotch. In fact, Scotch whisky remains the biggest part of the market and, although a small number of whisky mega-producers dominate, no single company has overall control. This fragmented market makes for interesting and innovative drinks, with distilleries competing with new recipes and processes. And there is one area where whisky production is at its most fascinating, with huge excitement surrounding new Scotches and bourbons: it's the Asia Pacific region, powered by Japanese distilleries and Australian small-batchers.

As the amber spirit continues to find its way into the very best cocktails, dive bars and home liquor cabinets, let's raise a glass to those illustrious monks who, hundreds of years ago, performed a true miracle: they turned beer into whisky, and the world has never been the same since.

THE SCIENCE OF WHISKY: MASH IT UP

Each iteration of this hallowed spirit is made the same way, via a gloopy mash of grains, from barley, rye and wheat to corn, all mixed with yeast for fermentation. It's a process whisky shares with beer until its distillation in a copper still.

Although there are myriad ways to mish your mash, broadly speaking, the mash is a sort of porridge made with malted grain (malting involves a spa day for grain, the luxury of a warm soak to make it sprout, and then dried off with hot air – or peat smoke – to halt the germination process). The porridge is boiled with fresh water for a couple of hours, and then cooled to a stodgy consistency. What's left – the mash – is then dolloped into a fermenting tank, yeast is added and then, through a magical process and a variety of temperatures and timings, a steeped and potent liquid – wort – is created. It's this liquid, full of alcohol and sugars and teeming with flavouring compounds, that is then distilled and – almost always – stored in charred white oak casks to mature for at least 18 months, but usually much longer.

It's then bottled and ready to drink neat or mixed into a cocktail that underlines its complex flavours. The opportunity for near-infinite variation in the process – type and quality of grain, the time it takes to steep and ferment, minute temperature changes, distillation equipment and the twinkle in a whisky-maker's eye – creates a huge variety of delicious whiskies and bourbons.

The World's Best Whiskies & Bourbons

TRIED AND TESTED, MIXED, SIPPED, SPILT AND MOPPED UP: THESE ARE THE WORLD'S VERY BEST WHISKIES AND BOURBONS, FROM STEADFAST MEGABRANDS TO YOUNG INDIE UPSTARTS.

FOR THE GREATEST OF ALL TIME

GLENMORANGIE SIGNET

The ultimate gift for your whisky-loving dad, grandma
or parole officer; if you have a single malt fan in your
life, this would be the gift that delights. Dark fruit,
roasted malt, dark chocolate and doughnut sugar shine
out in this bold, soft and utterly delicious drop.
Glenmorangie's Signet is made via a fastidious and
time-consuming process, is twice distilled (with a
delicate barley usually used in craft beer-making), and
rumours are that some of its blend comes from whisky
that is 35–40 years old. It's award-winning, of course,
pricey (but great value) and looks fantastic on your
home bar.

FOR OLD-SCHOOL DEVOTEES OF A CLASSIC

JOHNNIE WALKER BLACK LABEL

There's a reason whisky drinkers order Johnnie Walker
Black Label at the bar – it's by far the world's most
dependable depiction of the spirit: peaty, smoky and
big tasting, but surprisingly smooth and a perfect sipper.
That said, it comes alive in cocktails, bringing that
house-on-fire taste to any recipe, and works hard to
temper sweet and powerfully citrus drinks. And while
it might have retirement-gift vibes for some, it remains
one of the world's best examples of whisky production.
And no wonder – it's a blend of almost 40 whiskies –
its perfection isn't an accident.

FOR UPSTATE RULE-BREAKERS

BRIGHT LIGHTS, BIG BOURBON

Upstate New York is the gorgeous bohemian playground of NYC's rich and famous; it's all apple-bobbing in orchards, film festivals, vintage stores, and the famous Hudson distillery, a handful of grain's throw from the magnificent Hudson River. Pioneering craft distiller Ralph Erenzo had the idea for a small distillery in the region in 2003, but had to challenge the government for permission to do it. In fact, Erenzo is thought to have paved the way for hundreds of new distilleries across the US. Although Hudson is now owned by Scottish family whisky-makers William Grant & Sons, little has changed: Bright Lights, Big Bourbon is a fantastic, bold spirit made from New York state corn.

FOR MARVELLOUS MELBURNIANS

STARWARD LEFT-FIELD SINGLE MALT AUSTRALIAN WHISKY

This marvellous Melbourne-based, award-winning Australian distillery, Starward, has been creating and casking delicious whiskies and more since 2007. The brand was founded by Italian-Australian David Vitale and inspired by Australia's feverishly cool food scene. To create Left-Field, the Starward team have used grain that's just a day's drive from the distillery and French oak casks that once housed Australia's boldest and brightest red wines. What's more, Melbourne's turbulent climate seems to speed up the maturation.

FOR CELTIC PUNK CHRISTMAS LOVERS

THE POGUES IRISH WHISKEY

Imagine if the Celtic punk band, bad-boy megastars and Christmas-season-playlist-haunters The Pogues were pickled by master whiskey-maker Frank McHardy in West Cork. The Pogues Irish Whiskey is the product of this nightmarish dream but – as it turns out – it's fascinating. McHardy has used West Cork's cool mesothermal microclimate, a very high malt content, bourbon casks and the crossed-eyed spirit of The Pogues themselves to create this drop. The Pogues, who were thought to be comfortably retired on 'Fairytale of New York', are now enjoying being on the lips of whiskey fans the world over. What's more, The Pogues Irish Whiskey is an award-winner. Punk spirit, pickled.

FOR THE MOST LOYAL METALLICA FANS

BLACKENED AMERICAN WHISKEY

This brandy-barrel-finished American whiskey, known as Blackened, is named after the standout track from Metallica's 1988 LP … *And Justice For All*. It's a collaboration with late master distiller Dave Pickerell and the band itself: a delicious blend of bourbon and rye, treated to the sounds of Metallica in its maturation process. If it sounds crazy, it is, but the sonic-enhancement process – blaring the deep sounds of the band at Spanish brandy barrels – is thought to vibrate the liquid contents.

FOR FEMINISTS FIRMLY OFF THE WAGON

FEW STRAIGHT BOURBON WHISKEY

This utterly delicious craft spirit was born in Evanston, Illinois, just outside Chicago (a rarity, as almost all whiskey and bourbon production is traditionally based in Kentucky), and one-time home to the Women's Christian Temperance Union. Understandably, achieving a distiller's licence was tricky, but owner Paul Hletko pulled it off in 2011, and named his brand FEW after local US feminist icon Frances Elizabeth Willard.

FOR WHOM SLOW AND STEADY WINS THE RACE

BUFFALO TRACE KENTUCKY STRAIGHT BOURBON WHISKEY

Created and casked at one of the oldest distilleries in Kentucky, Buffalo Trace uses its impressive history and expertise to make one heck of a delicious bourbon. Launched in 2011, Trace has had a slow and steady rise to fame, occupying a lucrative (although not too exciting) middle market of easy sippers and mixers. There are no bells and whistles, no salacious brewing stories to lean back on – instead, there is a boring commitment to quality, and it's this confident that simplicity makes Buffalo Trace the perfect spirit.

FOR THE BILL MURRAY FAN CLUB

SUNTORY TOKI

Beloved indie movie *Lost in Translation* (2003) charts the startlingly brief relationship between an aging Hollywood star and a young woman (Scarlett Johansson) who are somewhat thrown together in Tokyo. Bill Murray plays the aging star battling moroseness and jet lag to film a TV commercial for Suntory, the Japanese spirit brand. Since the film's release, Japanese whisky has become one of the world's most popular drops, with Suntory's Yamazaki, Hibiki and Hakushu as the forerunners. But it's the blended Suntory Toki that's a more affordable entry point into the world of Japanese whiskies. Thank goodness, then, that it's delicious. Expect notes of vanilla, thyme, honey, green apple, pink grapefruit and bitter herbs.

FOR UNEXPLAINED MYSTERY LOVERS

BULLEIT STRAIGHT BOURBON WHISKEY

The mysterious disappearance of bourbon-mad tavern keeper Augustus Bulleit in the 1830s almost ended the story of this delicious bourbon before it had even begun. Somehow, the special recipe he created survived and, 150 years later, descendants of Augustus set about conjuring it into reality. Based in Kentucky (of course), Bulleit is a subtly spicy bourbon with an impressively smooth finish – almost, but not quite, a rye whiskey. Think vanilla, honey and toasted spice.

FOR MALTED MONKEYS

MONKEY SHOULDER BLENDED SCOTCH

This little monkey's delicious Blended Scotch is blended specifically for mixing, but its flavour profile is far more interesting than its primary use implies. It's packed with orange zest, honey and vanilla notes with a comforting maltiness and a warm hug of spiced oak. Monkey is relatively new on the block; it was casked in Scotland by William Grant & Sons in 2003 and enjoyed an almost immediate cult following.

FOR THOSE WHO LIKE IT SPICY

RITTENHOUSE STRAIGHT RYE WHISKEY

Pleasantly peppery, this award-winning, spicy little number is bottled-in-bond, the age-old North American best-in-show production process designed to preserve the quality of whiskey. Accordingly, Rittenhouse Rye is made from just one grain harvest, and one distillery, and the quality of RR speaks for itself. It's fruity, with dark berry undertones and a sweetness that presents after a peppery start. A perfect sipping whiskey and beloved by bartenders around the world, Rittenhouse is made at Heaven Hill in Louisville, Kentucky, the largest indie – and family-run – bourbon distillery in the world.

FOR SMALL-BATCH INDIE LOVERS

NOAH'S MILL BOURBON

Kentucky, home of the Willett family – one of the oldest whiskey- and bourbon-makers in the state – and their distillery founded in 1936, just three years after Prohibition. The Willetts' first barrel was completed one year later, and the distillery now produces more than 10 brands of whiskey and bourbon and is credited with helping keep Kentucky's bourbon industry alive when times were a little less kind for the amber spirit. It's Willett's blended and award-winning Noah's Mill that excites with notes of walnut, prune and florals featuring lavender, mint, cinnamon and burnt caramel.

FOR FANS OF SCOTTISH-JAPANESE FUSION

NIKKA COFFEY GRAIN WHISKY

Masataka Taketsuru, thought of as the 'father of Japanese whisky', studied the art of booze-making in Scotland in the early 1900s. He returned to Japan in 1920; his notebooks from Glasgow University became a whisky how-to guide, and it was under Taketsuru's expert stewardship that the Yamazaki distillery, the country's first whisky production site that was owned by the company that became Suntory, was built in 1923. After founding Nikka Whisky, Taketsuru imported Scottish 'Coffey' pot stills. Today, Nikka Coffey Grain Whisky is still made the old-fashioned way.

Essential Whisky Gadgetry

DON'T KNOW YOUR HAWTHORNE STRAINER FROM YOUR JIGGER? THE RIGHT GADGETS ELEVATE A WHISKY COCKTAIL FROM NICE AND TASTY TO BRAIN-NUMBINGLY EXCELLENT.

IMPRESSIVE TOOLS

Invest in your own at-home whisky palace with a range of impressive cocktail-making tools. Start off simple: shaker, jigger, blender, Hawthorne strainer and ice bucket. Here's what you'll need to keep it minimal:

JUICER

For extracting the pure juice from fruit or ginger, etc. – rather than adding the pith, skin, seeds and fibres, as with a smoothie – you'll need a juicer. It's an investment, sure, but you'll end up with the next level in cocktails – and think of all the green-juice Instagram opportunities.

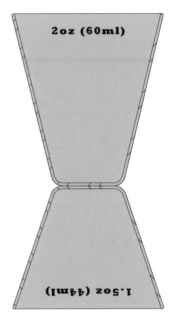

JIGGER

A toolbox essential. The jigger is the standard measure for spirits and liqueurs and is available in many different sizes. Heavy metallic jiggers look the part, but plastic or glass versions also do the job. If you don't have a jigger, or a single shot glass as a stand-in, use an egg cup – at least then your ratios will be right, even if your shots might be a little over-generous. Failing that, cross your fingers and free-pour your drinks.

MIXING GLASS

A simple, sturdy straight-sided glass (also known as a Boston) – or a straight-sided pint glass that tapers out – used for cocktails that need stirring with a bar spoon rather than shaking or to allow for extra volume when attached to the can of your shaker (to make two or more drinks at a time). The two halves are locked together and you shake until the drink is chilled, then a Hawthorne strainer can be used to strain the drink into a glass.

CITRUS SQUEEZER

A clever and pleasingly simple invention: the citrus squeezer is a hand press for citrus fruits. Chop the fruit in half, place in the squeezer, then press with all your might so the juice runs out and the pips and pith stay behind. Always use fresh citrus juices. If you don't have a squeezer, squeeze the juice through your fingers, catching the pips as you go.

SHAKER

Sometimes known as the Boston Shaker, it's the home mixer's silver bullet. This is your single most important piece of kit as very few cocktails are possible without one. The classic metallic model has three main parts: a base, known as the 'can' (a tall, tumbler shape that tapers out) and a tight-fitting funnel top with built-in strainer,

onto which a small cap fits (which can also be used as a jigger). It's brilliantly straightforward, and like all the finest tools, it pays to keep it scrupulously clean. If you can't get your hands on one, consider using a large glass jar with a lid and a waterproof seal.

HAWTHORNE STRAINER

The showy-looking strainer, trimmed with a spring, that comes in handy when your shaker's built-in version isn't up to the job. Place on a glass and pour the cocktail through it, or hold up against the cocktail can or mixing glass and pour from a height. Wash immediately after use, especially if you're straining a cream-based cocktail. A fine tea strainer does the job brilliantly, but the classic Hawthorne really looks the part.

BLENDER

Essential for fruity little numbers. Unless you're using something powerful like a Nutribullet or Vitamix, most domestic blenders find ice a little difficult, so it's best to use crushed ice in blender cocktails, rather than cubes or rocks. Add your ingredients first, then the ice, and start off on a slow speed before turning it up to max. No need to strain. Once the consistency is super smooth, pour into a glass and serve.

CUTTING BOARD AND KNIFE

Simple, but essential. Keep the board clean, the knife super sharp and practise your peeling skills: the aim is to avoid as much white pith as possible, leaving just the peel that is studded with aromatic oils.

ICE BUCKET

The centrepiece of your home bar; it can be simple, functional and slightly retro or the full plastic pineapple. An insulated ice bucket means your ice cubes will keep their shape for longer, and a good set of tongs adds a touch of class.

A Guide

to

Glasses

STEER AWAY FROM ORDINARY GLASSWARE TO
SERVE YOUR DRINKS. THE HOME MIXER SHOULD
TAKE A LITTLE PRIDE IN WHAT THEY PRESENT –
AND INVEST IN SOME UPSCALE COUPES,
TUMBLERS AND HIGHBALLS. BECAUSE WHY NOT?

COUPE

The short, trumpet-shaped glass is perfect for Champagne or sparkling wines and is a respectable martini-glass alternative; a coupe makes almost any short cocktail feel just that little bit fancier. (**Fig. 1**)

MARTINI

Cocktail culture's most iconic glass: the refined stem and cone-shaped glass flares out to create a large, shallow recess. Somehow, it loses its ability not to slosh out its contents as the evening wears on. (**Fig. 2**)

MOSCOW MULE MUG

The iconic copper mug, traditionally used for a Moscow Mule or Mojito, forms a refreshing-looking, frosty condensation when packed with ice.

FIG. 1

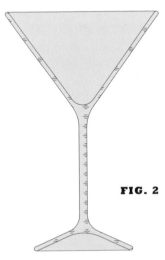

FIG. 2

BOSTON GLASS

The twin brother of the straight-sided pint glass, swapped at birth. Great for mixing in or for using locked into the can of your shaker. (**Fig. 3**)

SHOT GLASS

Short and simple. Pour, drink, slam down. Done. Also doubles as a jigger.

HIGHBALL

A tall glass, with a thick and sturdy bottom, which holds 225–350 ml (8–12 oz) of perfectly mixed booze. (**Fig. 4**)

TUMBLER

The short, straight-sided glass perfect for short or single-shot drinks. As with most good barware, it's best to pick one with a heavy bottom. (**Fig. 5**)

FIG. 4

FIG. 3

FIG. 5

COLLINS GLASS

The skinny, usually straight-sided version of the highball. (**Fig. 6**)

TIKI MUG

The tiki mug was born in mid-20th-century American tiki bars and is attributed to the founding father of tiki culture, Donn Beah, and his bar Don the Beachcomber. It's a tall, wonky-looking ceramic mug with a face like an Easter Island statue, or moai. (**Fig. 7**)

CHAMPAGNE FLUTE

The flute-shaped glass used for Champagne cocktails, Bellinis and Mimosas. (**Fig. 8**)

FIG. 6

FIG. 7

FIG. 8

Tricks
of the
Trade

IT'S NOT WHAT YOU HAVE, IT'S WHAT YOU DO
WITH IT. THERE'S MORE TO MAKING A WHISKY
OR BOURBON COCKTAIL THAN GRABBING A
SHAKER AND FURIOUSLY BASHING ONE OUT. LIKE
ALL THE BEST THINGS, THERE'S AN ART TO IT.

How To Do It

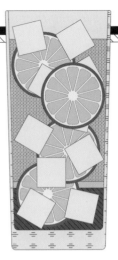

SHAKE

How long exactly should you shake the perfect concoction? No one can agree. Some say 15 seconds of brisk shaking, others say less. This book is going out on a limb and settling on a short and sharp 7 seconds. Any longer could dilute the drink a little too much, affecting potency. In your drink-making process, there should be no bottle flipping or sparkler lighting, although a little lemon and lime juggling wouldn't go amiss.

CHILL

If you have room, clear a shelf in your freezer and keep your cocktail glasses on ice, or pack them full of cubes to throw away when the glass is chilled.

POTENCY

All cocktails are potent, but some are more potent than others. Each drink should seek to achieve a perfect balance of flavours and can attempt differing levels of intensity, but shouldn't get you drunk – at least not on its own. Perfect measurements really matter.

STIR

Whip out your bar spoon and your mixing glass, and stir drinks gently and deftly with ice to chill the concoction. When condensation forms on the outside of the glass, it's ready to go.

THE LOOK

Fresh garnishes, squeaky-clean glasses, clear, purified ice and a perfect balance of colours and visible textures are essential.

AROMATICS

Your drink should not only taste good, but also smell nothing less than amazing. Bitters, fresh juices and citrus peels packed with fragrant oils help achieve this.

HOW TO PUT YOUR BACK BAR TOGETHER

Apart from a collection of the world's best whiskies and bourbons – from Johnnie Walker Black Label to delicious single-batch, artisanal bourbons – and your own homemade infusions, create a backbar with a mix of strong, clean and classic spirits, the odd special buy and a few rarities. You don't need to stock up on fine vintage spirits for cocktails – their subtler qualities are lost in the mixing – but you do need to invest in something of quality. Pick a sturdy, deep-tasting bourbon rather than an aged malt. International brands Monkey Shoulder, Knob Creek, FEW and Bulleit Bourbon are all strong contenders.

WHISKY AND SCOTCH

The smoky, earthy one. Aged in oak barrels for at least 3 years, Scottish whisky (in style or provenance), or Scotch, was traditionally made from malted barley, but contemporary recipes are a little more experimental with the grain. 'Single grain' implies the whisky was made at a single distillery (not necessarily using a single type of grain), while 'single malt' means it employs a malted grain – again, made at a single distillery. Blends are just that: a fusion of two or more whiskies, some malted, some not – and account for most of the whisky made in the misty nation.

WHISKEY

The Irish and North American version, smoother and less fiery than its Scottish twin. 'Irish' whiskey can only be made in Ireland, but whisky itself can be from anywhere (although only the Irish and the Americans spell 'whiskey' with an 'e').

RYE

In the States, rye whiskey must be made from a majority (51 per cent or more) rye mash, be unblended, and be aged in charred new oak barrels for at least two years. In Canada, things are a little different: rye whiskey is a more general term and might have little rye in it, if at all (although it will be delicious).

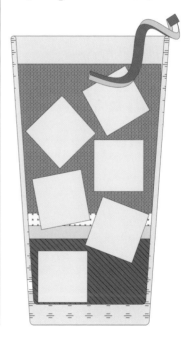

American rye whiskey is a spicy, peppery drop and therefore fascinating in cocktails.

BOURBON

Bourbon is a subset of whiskey, a cute, younger American cousin that's often a little sweeter and smoother (and has great teeth). A majority corn mash makes for more sugar; bourbon is often the whisky fan's starter spirit and has earned itself a delightful place in cocktail recipes.

VERMOUTH

The fortified wine packed with botanicals, in sweet and dry versions – and also in 'blanc',

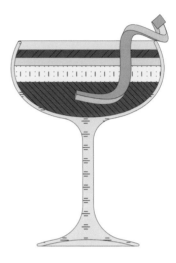

a sort of Goldilocks version, in between. Get them all and keep them refrigerated after opening.

TEQUILA

The agave-based brain melter. Unaged (or aged for no more than 60 days in steel containers), silver (*blanco*) tequila is an essential part of your backbar. Gold tequila is sweet and smooth, coloured and flavoured with caramel; *reposado* ('rested') tequila, aged in wood-lined tanks or barrels, brings a smoky undertone to your mixes.

VODKA

Stolichnaya, Smirnoff and Absolut are all reliable brands, while the more expensive Crystal Head vodka – encased in a skull-shaped bottle – certainly looks the part.

GIN

Mother's ruin, hell broth, giggle juice, the quick flash of lightning. Make sure your gin is premium enough for sipping and remember

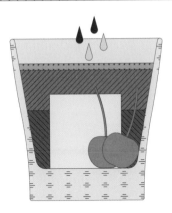

to mix the subtler spirits with mixers. Save the flavourful ones for cocktails that let the botanicals sing out – like a dry Gin Martini or a Gin Old Fashioned. The perfect backbar would have one small-batch, handcrafted premium gin and a couple of upscale contenders for mixing.

RUM

Rum is the liquor sailors drank to ward off scurvy. Cheap rum, that is. Invest a little in an upscale number like Zacapa or Brugal Añejo and you'll feel less *Pirates of the Caribbean* and more luxury yacht. Light rum, milder in flavour, is easier to mix.

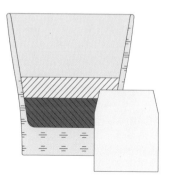

TRIPLE SEC AND ORANGE LIQUEUR

A backbar essential, triple sec (or a high-quality orange liqueur like Cointreau) is made from the dried peel of sweet and bitter oranges and has a deep, rich flavour that is the perfect element for many cocktails.

CAMPARI AND APEROL

Sharp, ruby-red bitters that pep up cocktails and form the basis of the Negroni and Americano. They are really quite life-changing mixed with soda water and chilled sparkling wine.

CASSIS

Invest in a good-quality crème de cassis or crème de mûre: dark, berry-flavoured liqueurs for Kirs, Kir Royales and more besides – they're the perfect sweetener in pared-down recipes. Mix a drop of cassis into a G & T to give it a sweet berry kick.

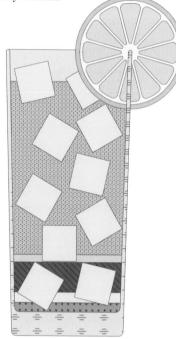

SYRUP

A cocktail essential. Simple syrup – aka gomme or sugar syrup – is liquid sugar and, mixed part for part with sharp citrus juices, it brings a delightfully sweet-sour note to a recipe. Buy a premium version of simple syrup (Monin is a good, decent brand) or make your own. Agave syrup is a naturally occurring syrup that is available in raw, light and amber – light is best for most cocktails as it has a clean, simple taste.

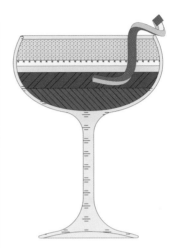

BITTERS

Angostura bitters (Venezuelan-by-way-of-Trinidad-and-Tobago aromatics) are an essential element of the backbar. Said to be a cure for hiccups, the part-herbal, part-alcoholic tinctures are highly aromatic, giving cocktails a depth of taste and colouring white spirits a subtle sunrise pink. Bitters and cordial producers Fee Brothers (est. 1863) is another good brand to start with: their whisky-barrel-aged bitters with rhubarb and plum flavours are particularly mouth-caving.

MIXERS

They say no one uses cola as a mixer anymore. No one (although you're permitted a splash in a Long Island Iced Tea). But make sure you have a ginger beer or ale, chilled sparkling water or soda, prosecco, cava or Champagne and freshly squeezed citrus juices, premium cloudy lemonade, cranberry juice, elderflower cordial, coconut water and – always – a truckload of ice.

Syrups And How To Make Them

SUPERCHARGE SIMPLE (BUT GOOD-QUALITY) BOOZE WITH YOUR OWN INFUSIONS OR CREATE A SIMMERED-DOWN REDUCTION TO ADD A POWER PUNCH OF FLAVOUR.

SYRUPS AND REDUCTIONS

The sweet stuff. Taking the edge off sour citrus flavours and softening the taste of bitter spirits, a dash of sugar syrup can transform a drink, turning the toughest liquor into soda pop. Flavoured syrup adds a level of complexity a fresh ingredient just can't achieve. And it's very nearly foolproof to make – start with the Simple Syrup recipe below, graduate to the flavoured recipes and then begin to create your own. You could always buy them ready-made, but they're so simple, so you really don't need to.

It's not essential to use unrefined sugar, but it's tastier, chemical-free and – used in all your cocktail recipes and syrup-making – lends a wobbly irregularity to proceedings that could only be handmade.

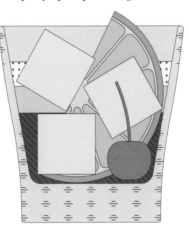

SIMPLE SYRUP

Makes enough dashes for
approximately 15 drinks

INGREDIENTS

200 ml (7 oz) water
100 g (3½ oz) demerara, cane
or granulated sugar
1 tbsp golden syrup or corn syrup
(optional)

EQUIPMENT Non-stick
saucepan, wooden spoon, 200 ml
(7 oz) Kilner (Mason) jar or glass
bottle with a stopper and a funnel

METHOD Boil the water in a
non-stick saucepan and gently add
the sugar. Reduce the heat and stir
constantly with a wooden spoon
for 3–5 minutes, until all the sugar
is dissolved and the syrup is clear.
Turn off the heat and leave to cool.
While still runny, pour into a
sterilised Kilner jar or bottle.
Adding a spoonful of syrup to the
cooled mixture now will help keep
the syrup smooth. Store in the
fridge for up to 6 weeks.

RHUBARB, GINGER & STAR ANISE SYRUP

Makes enough dashes for
approximately 15 drinks

INGREDIENTS

200 ml (7 oz) water
100 g (3½ oz) demerara, cane
or granulated sugar
2 rhubarb stalks, cut into chunks
1 tablespoon grated fresh ginger
1 star anise, slightly crushed
15 ml (½ oz) lemon juice, freshly
squeezed
1 tablespoon golden syrup
or corn syrup (optional)

EQUIPMENT Non-stick
saucepan, wooden spoon,
muslin, heatproof bowl,
200 ml (7 oz) Kilner (Mason)
jar or glass bottle with a stopper
and a funnel

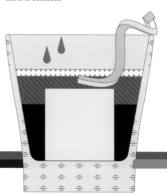

METHOD Boil the water in a non-stick saucepan. Add the sugar, rhubarb, ginger, star anise and lemon juice. Turn down the heat and stir constantly with a wooden spoon for 3–5 minutes, until all the sugar is dissolved. Turn off the heat and leave to cool. While the syrup is still runny, pass it through a muslin-lined strainer into a heatproof bowl, then decant it into a Kilner jar or bottle. Adding a spoonful of syrup now will help keep the mixture smooth. Store in the fridge for up to 6 weeks.

SPICED BROWN SUGAR SYRUP

Makes enough dashes for approximately 15 drinks

INGREDIENTS

200 ml (7 oz) water
100 g (3½ oz) dark brown sugar
1 tablespoon grated fresh ginger
dash of lemon juice, freshly squeezed
1 tablespoon golden syrup or corn syrup (optional)

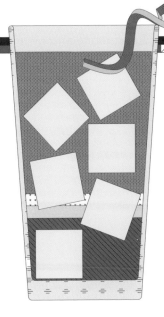

EQUIPMENT Non-stick saucepan, wooden spoon, muslin, heatproof bowl, 200 ml (7 oz) Kilner (Mason) jar or glass bottle with a stopper and a funnel

METHOD Boil the water in a non-stick saucepan. Add the sugar and ginger. Turn down the heat and stir constantly with a wooden spoon for 3–5 minutes, until all the sugar is dissolved. Turn off the heat and add the lemon juice and leave to cool. When cooled, strain the syrup into a Kilner jar. Adding a spoonful of syrup will help keep the mixture smooth.

BIG CARDAMOMMA'S HOUSE SYRUP

Makes enough dashes for
approximately 15 drinks

INGREDIENTS

200 ml (7 oz) water
100 g (3½ oz) granulated sugar
8–10 cardamom pods, smashed
lightly so the pod breaks open
2 cinnamon sticks
pinch of crushed chilli (optional)
1 tbsp golden syrup or corn syrup
(optional)

EQUIPMENT Non-stick
saucepan, wooden spoon, 200 ml
(7 oz) Kilner (Mason) jar or glass
bottle with a stopper and a funnel

METHOD Boil the water in
a non-stick saucepan and gently
add the sugar, cardamom,
cinnamon sticks, and a pinch
of chilli, if you fancy. Turn down
the heat and stir constantly for
3–5 minutes, until all the sugar
is dissolved. Turn off the heat and
leave to cool. While the syrup is
still runny, pour it into a Kilner
jar or bottle. Adding a spoonful of
syrup to the cooled mixture now
will help keep the
syrup smooth.
Store in the
fridge for up
to 6 weeks.

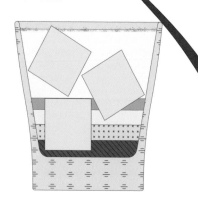

PINE TIP SYRUP

Makes enough dashes for approximately 15 drinks

INGREDIENTS

200 ml (7 oz) water
100 g (3½ oz) demerara, cane or granulated sugar
handful of freshly picked pine tips (the little bright green leaves from spruce or pine trees, rather than the dark green, older leaves)
1 tbsp golden syrup or corn syrup (optional)

EQUIPMENT Non-stick saucepan, wooden spoon, 200 ml (7 oz) Kilner (Mason) jar or glass bottle with stopper and a funnel

METHOD Boil the water in a non-stick saucepan and gently add the sugar and pine tips. Reduce the heat and stir constantly with a wooden spoon for 3–5 minutes, until all the sugar is dissolved and the syrup is clear. Turn off the heat and leave to cool. While still runny, pour into a sterilised Kilner (Mason) jar or funnel into a sterilised glass bottle with stopper. Adding a spoonful of syrup to the cooled mixture will help keep the syrup smooth. Store in the fridge for up to 6 weeks.

Other Flavoured Syrups

Using Simple Syrup (page 38) as the base, make your own infusions, tweaking amounts to taste according to the potency of your flavourings. A sprig or two for rosemary syrup should do it, whereas mint syrup needs a good handful. It's not an exact science.

Brown Sugar, Molasses Basil & Lime
Cinnamon
Ginger & Cardamom Honey
Ground Coffee Mint
Pink Peppercorn Rhubarb Rosemary
Sage
Vanilla Pod (Bean)

Sours

Sours – citrus-based mixes that can include sugar syrup and egg white – cut through the gloopy sweetness of liqueurs. Shaken up with egg white and sugar syrup, a hit of fresh lemon and lime juice, or grapefruit and blood orange, they are the fizzing top note of recipes like the classic Whiskey Sour. But a simple half measure of lemon juice stirred through any sweet concoction will also do the trick, turning a grandma's snifter into something otherworldly.

SIMPLE SOUR MIX

INGREDIENTS

15 ml (½ oz) lemon juice, freshly
squeezed
15 ml (½ oz) lime juice, freshly
squeezed

METHOD Mix both juices
and deploy.

CLASSIC SOUR MIX

INGREDIENTS

15 ml (½ oz) lemon juice, freshly
squeezed
15 ml (½ oz) lime juice, freshly
squeezed
15 ml (½ oz) Simple Syrup
(page 38)
1 egg white or 3 tbsp aquafaba

METHOD Mix both juices,
sugar syrup and egg white/
aquafaba together and shake over
ice with your chosen spirit.

BLOODY SOUR MIX

INGREDIENTS

15 ml (½ oz) blood orange juice,
freshly squeezed

15 ml (½ oz) pink grapefruit juice,
freshly squeezed

METHOD Mix both juices
and deploy.

\\\\\\\\\\\\\\\\\\\\

BRINES

Brines: odd, salty infusions stolen
from olive, caper and pickle jars
add a savoury, acid kick to a
drink, cutting through sweetness
with more brute strength than
citrus. But adding brine to an
already hard, sharp liquor almost
underlines its power. Olive brine
mixed with a Whiskey Sour lends
a deep, savoury kick; cornichons
and a drop of pickle juice add a
sharp, acrid note, seeming only to
increase whisky's firepower. The
best bit? It's like having a drink
and dinner in one, which, frankly,
allows time for more drinking.
There are no precise instructions
or quantities here – add your
choice of brine according to taste.

The Recipes

FROM ZINGY CLASSICS TO CONTEMPORARY
UPSTARTS SIZZLING WITH FLAVOUR – GET READY
TO SHAKE, MUDDLE AND STIR.

WHISKY SOUR

This classic short drink perfectly straddles the sweet-sour binary with sharp citrus flavour and sweet simple syrup that will liven up anything from your favourite premium bourbon to whatever firewater you nab on a late night booze run. It has an easy-on-the-eye orange hue and is drinkable in the extreme. Serve icy cold, of course.

INGREDIENTS

1	bourbon	60 ml (2 oz)
2	lemon juice, freshly squeezed	20 ml (⅔ oz)
3	Simple Syrup (page 38)	20 ml (⅔ oz)
4	orange wheel	½, to garnish
5	cocktail cherry	to garnish

EQUIPMENT Shaker, strainer

METHOD Shake the bourbon, lemon juice and simple syrup over ice until very cold. Strain into a glass filled with ice, add the garnish and serve.

GLASS TYPE:
TUMBLER
OR ROCKS

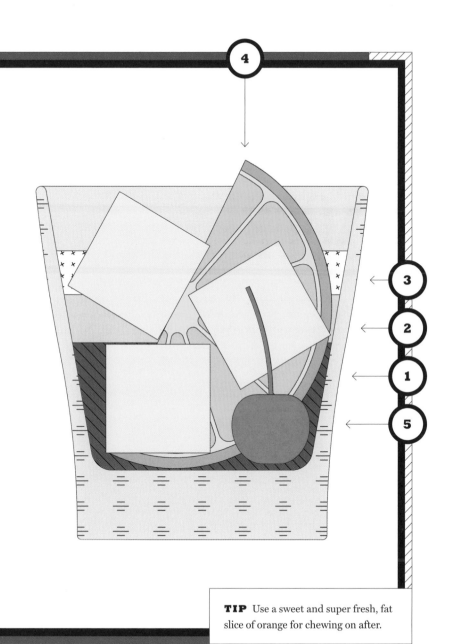

TIP Use a sweet and super fresh, fat slice of orange for chewing on after.

ICED TODDY

Spiced and iced, this cooled-down version of the hot hot hot classic Hot Toddy is delicious. Bring it briefly to the boil, let it cool and chill to create a refreshing cocktail with a pleasingly complex flavour profile.

INGREDIENTS (SERVES 6-8)

1	peels of 6 lemons and 1 orange	
2	fresh ginger, peeled and muddled, plus thinly sliced pieces to garnish	
3	cloves	5-6
4	cinnamon sticks	3-4
5	lemon juice, freshly squeezed	235 ml (8 oz)
6	orange juice, freshly squeezed	120 ml (4 oz)
7	jasmine teabags	3
8	honey	160 ml (5½ oz)
9	whisky	475 ml (16 oz)
10	cardamom or orange bitters	2 drops
11	orange twists	to garnish

EQUIPMENT Peeler, saucepan, fine sieve, pitcher

METHOD Briefly simmer the peels, ginger, spices, citrus juices, teabags and a cup of water in a saucepan. Add honey, let cool, strain, add whisky and bitters, chill and serve in a toddy glass and garnish with ginger slices and orange twists.

GLASS TYPE:
TODDY
OR TUMBLER

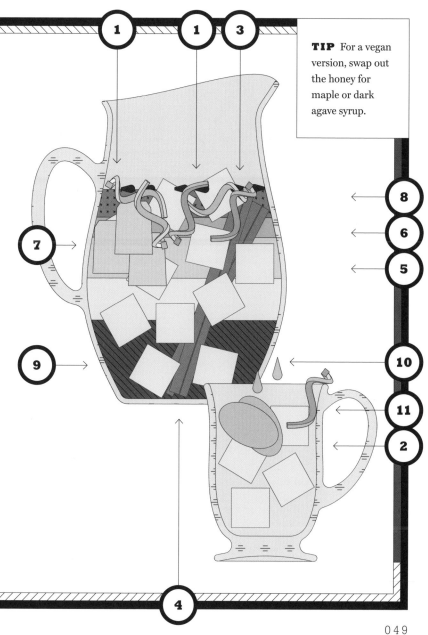

TIP For a vegan version, swap out the honey for maple or dark agave syrup.

THIRSTY COWBOY

Keep your cowboy well-lubricated with this easy, no-drama bourbon and beer cocktail. Use a dark, musty spirit to give this dude real depth and flavour and your favourite light craft lager rather than a strong ale to keep things firmly in the saddle.

INGREDIENTS

1	bourbon	60 ml (2 oz)
2	lemon juice, freshly squeezed	20 ml (⅔ oz)
3	Simple Syrup (page 38)	20 ml (⅔ oz)
4	premium chilled lager	330 ml (11¼ oz)
5	lime twist	to garnish

EQUIPMENT Shaker, strainer, bar spoon

METHOD Shake the bourbon, lemon juice and simple syrup over ice until very cold. Strain into a pint glass filled with ice, carefully top with lager and slowly stir. Garnish with a lime twist.

GLASS TYPE:
PINT

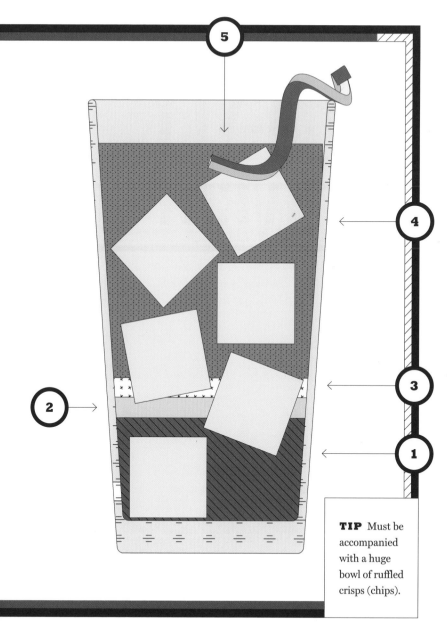

TIP Must be accompanied with a huge bowl of ruffled crisps (chips).

THE RATTLESNAKE

This once-forgotten classic is said to cure a rattlesnake bite – or kill the snake itself – and was first seen in print on London's Savoy Hotel cocktail list in 1930. It's a delightfully boozy drink that is tangy, sharp and creamy with an anise fragrance. It may not cure any emergency ailment whatsoever, but it will get you merry enough not to care.

INGREDIENTS

1	bourbon	45 ml (1½ oz)
2	egg white	1
3	lemon juice, freshly squeezed	dash
4	lime juice, freshly squeezed	dash
5	Simple Syrup (page 38)	10 ml (⅓ oz)
6	Pernod	to rinse

EQUIPMENT Shaker, fine mesh sieve

METHOD Dry shake the liquids (except the Pernod) until frothy. Then, add ice and shake again vigorously for a full 20 seconds. Rinse a chilled coupe with a quick splash of Pernod and discard. Strain through a fine mesh sieve and serve.

GLASS TYPE:
COUPE

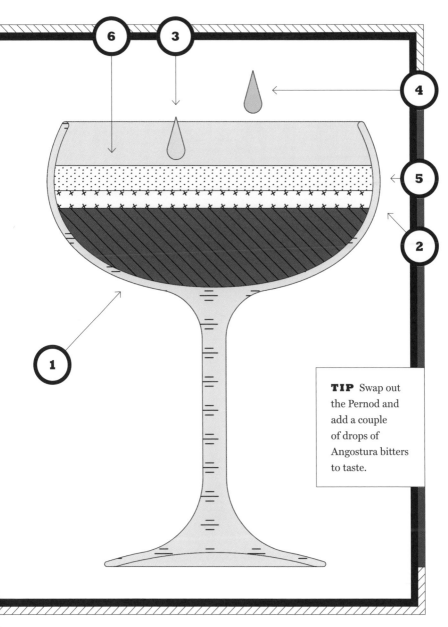

TIP Swap out
the Pernod and
add a couple
of drops of
Angostura bitters
to taste.

THE MANHATTAN

On the lips of partygoers since the late 1880s, New York City's infamous Manhattan Club crafted its signature cocktail with spicy American rye whiskey, sweet Italian vermouth and a devil-may-care attitude. This ruby-hued bourbon version is just a little softer and sweeter. Can also be served on the rocks.

INGREDIENTS

1	bourbon	60 ml (2 oz)
2	red (sweet) vermouth	30 ml (1 oz)
3	Angostura bitters	2 dashes
4	orange bitters	dash
5	lemon twist	to garnish
6	cocktail cherry	to garnish

EQUIPMENT Bar spoon, mixing glass, strainer

METHOD Stir the liquids in a mixing glass with ice to chill, strain into a chilled coupe and garnish with a lemon twist and cocktail cherry.

GLASS TYPE:
COUPE

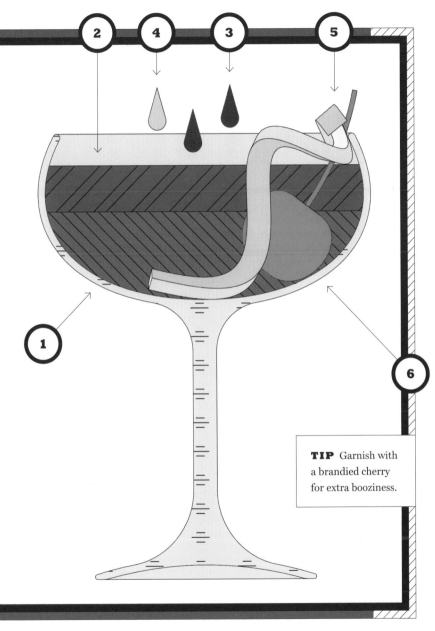

TIP Garnish with
a brandied cherry
for extra booziness.

OLD FASHIONED

The world's most delicious way to drink bourbon, this recipe is carefully calibrated to underline the beauty and quality of the spirit. In this way, bourbon, rye, even mezcal or gin could be used; but rich, dark bourbon is best. Make sure your orange twist is big enough to whack into your nose as you sip for full sensory overload.

INGREDIENTS

1	brown sugar	1 cube
2	Angostura bitters	2 dashes
3	soda water	splash
4	bourbon	60 ml (2 oz)
5	cocktail cherry	to garnish
6	oversized orange twist	to garnish

EQUIPMENT Muddler

METHOD Add the sugar cube to the glass, wet with bitters and a splash of soda water, muddle until dissolved, add one or two large pieces of ice, then pour over the bourbon. Add a cocktail cherry, and bend a large orange twist over the drink to release a little fragrant citrus oil before adding to the drink.

GLASS TYPE:
HEAVY
TUMBLER

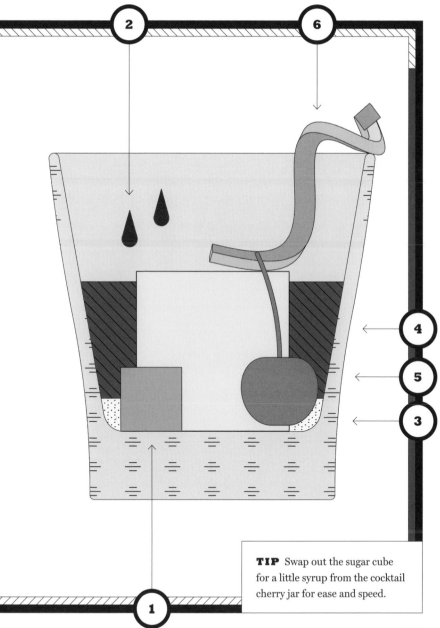

TIP Swap out the sugar cube for a little syrup from the cocktail cherry jar for ease and speed.

AMERICAN APERITIF

This simple, bourbon-powered aperitif uses ginger syrup and amaro liqueur for a dry, refreshingly bitter drink, a perfect alternative for those poor unfortunates who have over-imbibed on their summer Negronis.

INGREDIENTS

1	bourbon	60 ml (2 oz)
2	amaro-style liqueur	60 ml (2 oz)
3	ginger syrup	30 ml (1 oz)
4	lemon slice	to garnish

EQUIPMENT Mixing glass, bar spoon, strainer

METHOD Add the liquids to a mixing glass with ice, stir and strain into a tumbler over ice. Add lemon slice and serve.

GLASS TYPE:
HEAVY
TUMBLER

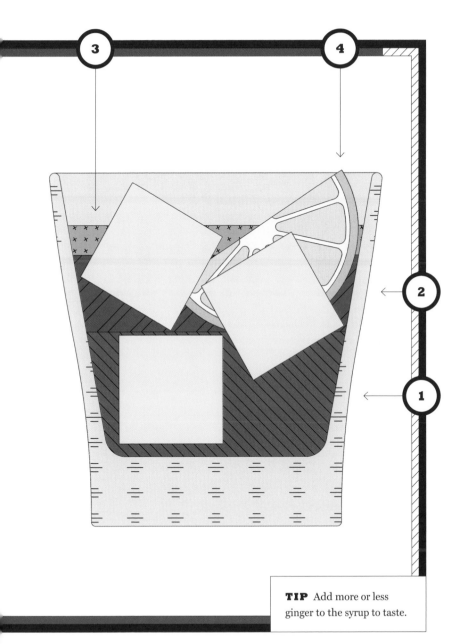

TIP Add more or less ginger to the syrup to taste.

Espresso Old Fashioned

The annoyingly refined, grown-up big brother to the Espresso Martini, this Espresso Old Fashioned is as powerful as it is simple. Just-made espresso from your local café raises this tasty pick me up to dizzying heights, but a good-quality home brew would also do the trick. Rye gives a little fiery kick, and a demerara-like, soft bourbon or blended whisky works perfectly.

INGREDIENTS

1	fresh espresso, room temperature	60 ml (2 oz) (about a double shot)
2	bourbon or rye	30 ml (1 oz)
3	Simple Syrup (page 38)	10 ml (⅓ oz)
4	Peychaud's bitters	dash
5	lemon twist	to garnish

EQUIPMENT Mixing glass, bar spoon, strainer

METHOD Add the liquids to a mixing glass and stir over ice until frosty. Strain into a tumbler over ice, lemon twist over drink, then discard.

GLASS TYPE:
HEAVY
TUMBLER

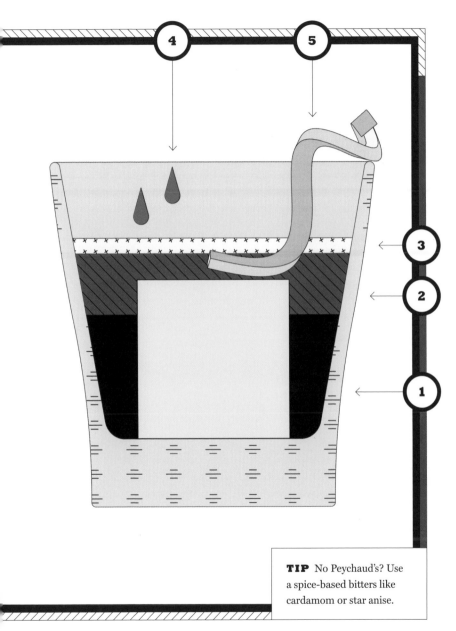

TIP No Peychaud's? Use a spice-based bitters like cardamom or star anise.

THE SAZERAC

This heady New Orleans cocktail is a twist on the classic Old Fashioned but with booze brand Sazerac's own anise-powered Peychaud's bitters, cognac and a little absinthe for summoning the spirit world. This 19th century concoction is a strong, complex herbal drink for late night scrying and spellcasting.

INGREDIENTS

1	brown sugar	1 cube
2	Peychaud's bitters	2 dashes
3	Angostura bitters	dash
4	bourbon or rye	30 ml (1 oz)
5	cognac	30 ml (1 oz)
6	absinthe	to rinse glass
7	lemon twist	to garnish

EQUIPMENT Muddler, mixing glass, strainer

METHOD Muddle the sugar, bitters and a dash of water in a mixing glass, add the bourbon, cognac and ice, and stir until frosty. Rinse a chilled tumbler with absinthe, discard the excess. Add one or two large pieces of ice and strain the drink into the glass. Garnish with a lemon twist.

GLASS TYPE:
HEAVY
TUMBLER

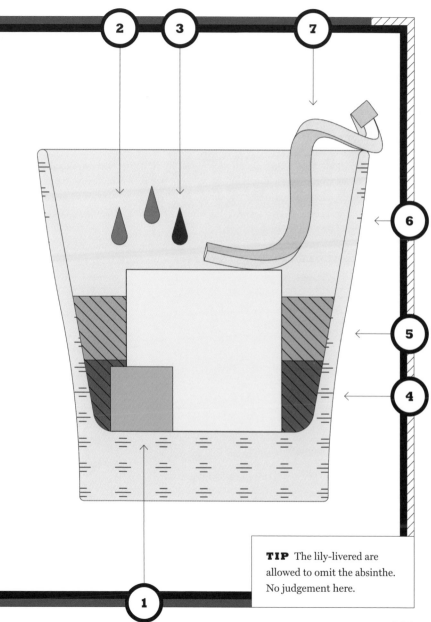

TIP The lily-livered are allowed to omit the absinthe. No judgement here.

WHISKY GRENADINE

This punch-like recipe leans heavily on grenadine and super fresh grapefruit for a refreshing, summery sipper that has just the right amount of tartness. Works just as well sloshed into a paper cup at a balcony BBQ as it does delicately poured into a crystal-cut rocks glass at your parents' wedding anniversary. You do you.

INGREDIENTS

1	pink grapefruit juice, freshly squeezed	60 ml (2 oz)
2	bourbon or rye	30 ml (1 oz)
3	red (sweet) vermouth	30 ml (1 oz)
4	grenadine	10 ml (⅓ oz)
5	lemon wheel	½, to garnish
6	cocktail cherry	to garnish

EQUIPMENT Shaker, strainer

METHOD Shake the liquids over ice until frosty and strain into a tumbler filled with ice. Garnish with a lemon wheel and a cocktail cherry.

GLASS TYPE:
HEAVY
TUMBLER

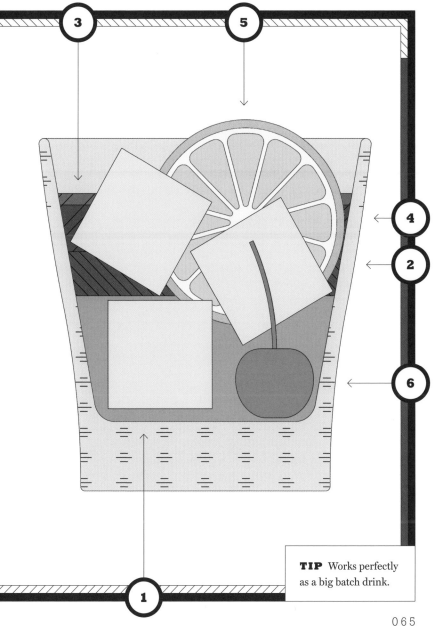

BOURBON SMASH

This simple, refreshing little recipe works well with gin, vodka, tequila and rum, but it's best with a rich, golden bourbon. Remember, this is a recipe that requires a slow hand. Heavy handed muddlers need not apply.

INGREDIENTS

1	mint leaves	5–6
2	lemon	½, cut lengthways
3	Simple Syrup (page 38)	10 ml (⅓ oz)
4	bourbon or rye	60 ml (2 oz)
5	Angostura bitters	dash

EQUIPMENT Muddler, mixing glass, strainer

METHOD Gently muddle the mint leaves, lemon and simple syrup in a mixing glass. Add the bourbon, then strain into a chilled tumbler, adding crushed ice, then the bitters, and garnishing with mint.

GLASS TYPE:
HEAVY
TUMBLER

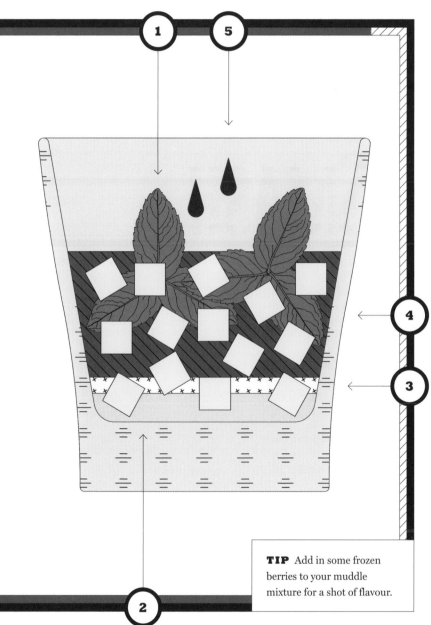

TIP Add in some frozen berries to your muddle mixture for a shot of flavour.

067

WATERMELON SUGAR

When pop star Harry Styles released his single 'Watermelon Sugar' in 2019, the world was alight with the mystery of what the term truly meant. Was it an ode to messily eating the most delicious summertime fruit in the world, or did he mean something else entirely? This cocktail – a watermelon, sugar and whisky muddle – is as fresh and surprising as Styles' clever wordplay: an oral explosion, if you will.

INGREDIENTS

1	whisky	60 ml (2 oz)
2	watermelon chunks (preferred)	3 large
	or fresh watermelon juice	60 ml (2 oz)
3	light brown sugar	1 teaspoon
4	fresh lime juice	15 ml (½ oz)

EQUIPMENT Mixing glass, muddler

METHOD Muddle the ingredients well in a mixing glass and pour into a tumbler over ice.

GLASS TYPE:
TUMBLER

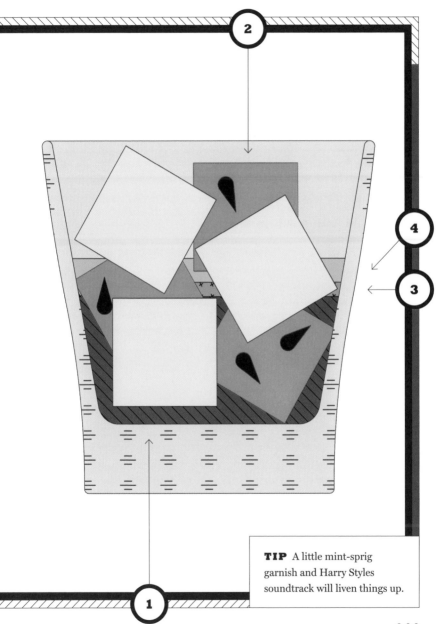

TIP A little mint-sprig garnish and Harry Styles soundtrack will liven things up.

RYE AMARO

With its amaro base, it has the feel of a complex Old Fashioned or Negroni. Amaro Montenegro has notes of rose, orange peel and cherry and, with its dark floral vibe, is heady. Want something less evocative of Nan's undies drawer? Swap it for something gently sweet like Amaro Nonino or Amaro CioCiaro rather than bitter Aperol or Campari.

INGREDIENTS

1	{	rye	30 ml (2 oz)
2	{	amaro	30 ml (2 oz)
3	{	brown sugar sage syrup (page 42)	10 ml (⅓ oz)
4	{	lemon juice, freshly squeezed	dash
5	{	Angostura bitters	2–3 drops
6	{	cocktail cherries	2–3, to garnish

EQUIPMENT Mixing glass, stirring spoon, strainer

METHOD Stir the rye, amaro, syrup and lemon juice over ice in a mixing glass, strain into a tumbler with rock ice, and add bitters and cherries to garnish.

GLASS TYPE:
TUMBLER

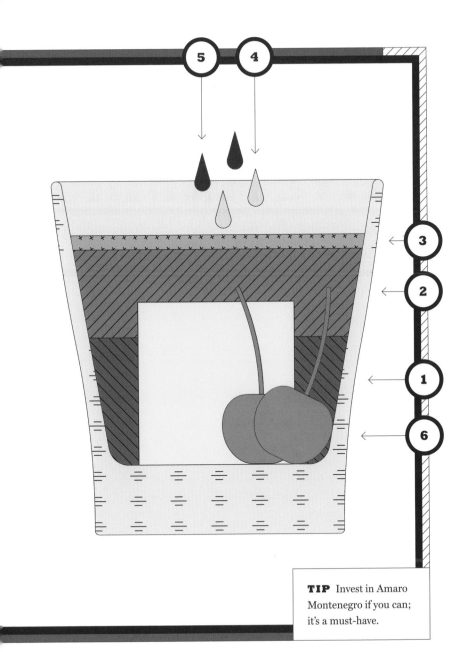

TIP Invest in Amaro Montenegro if you can; it's a must-have.

POSH SPICE

Although it seems gently sweet, this little number has body and heat. Use a smoky rye whiskey, and a little Big Cardamomma's House Syrup: a homemade spiced syrup with cinnamon, nutmeg and – of course – cardamom. Not such an innocent drink.

INGREDIENTS

1	rye	60 ml (2 oz)
2	Big Cardamomma's House Syrup (page 40)	10 ml (⅓ oz)
3	lemon juice, freshly squeezed	dash
4	fresh jalapeño	1 slice, to garnish

EQUIPMENT Shaker

METHOD Shake the liquids and serve either in a tumbler (over ice) or a chilled coupe. Garnish with jalapeño slice.

GLASS TYPE:
TUMBLER OR COUPE

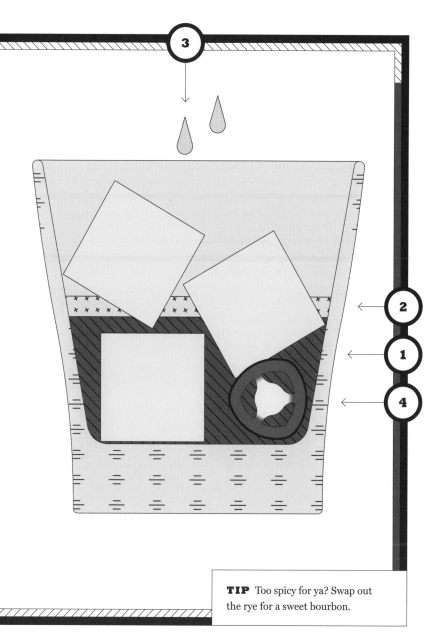

TIP Too spicy for ya? Swap out the rye for a sweet bourbon.

ADULT HORCHATA

This classic vegan Spanish nut-milk drink – and the popular Mexican rice-milk version – beloved of students recovering from a day of under-the-desk TikTok viewing and wedgies after school is as smooth as the day is long. The original recipes are delicious but tooth-dissolvingly sweet; this adult rendition relies on the natural sugars in the plant milk for a more grown-up taste. Of course, you can always add extra simple syrup if you want to play the kid. Serve icy cold.

INGREDIENTS

1	bourbon	60 ml (2 oz)
2	full-fat (whole) nut or rice milk	120 ml (4 oz)
3	vanilla extract	dash
4	Big Cardamomma's House Syrup (page 40)	10 ml (⅓ oz)

EQUIPMENT Shaker

METHOD Shake the ingredients over ice until very cold. Strain into a glass filled with ice and serve.

GLASS TYPE: HIGHBALL

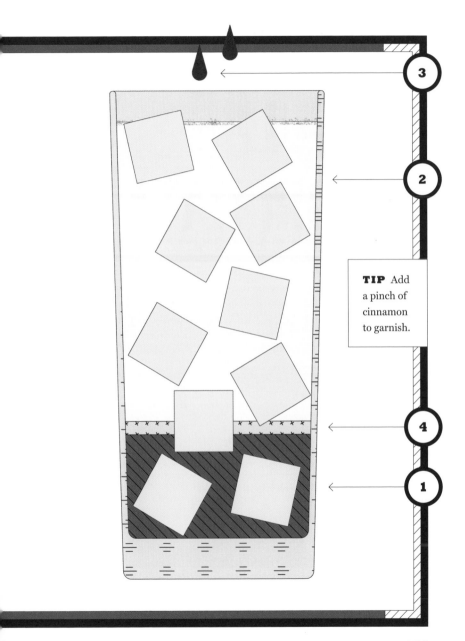

TIP Add a pinch of cinnamon to garnish.

TAYLOR'S VERSION

This adult version of Taylor Swift's Grande Caramel Non-fat Latte is an homage to the great singer-songwriter's favourite Starbucks order – and her impeccable taste. On the re-release of her album, *Red* (2021), Swifties were able to ask simply for 'Taylor's version' at their favourite 'bucks in celebration. Although this cooled-down iteration – a version of Taylor's version, if you will – has a delicious slug of whisky at its core, something Taylor has never openly advocated for but, hey, don't let that stop you. It's a delicious caramel White Russian – and it's vegan, too.

INGREDIENTS

1	bourbon	60 ml (2 oz)
2	oat milk	120 ml (4 oz)
3	caramel or Spiced Brown Sugar Syrup (page 39)	1 tablespoon

EQUIPMENT Shaker

METHOD Shake the bourbon, milk and syrup over ice until very cold. Strain into a glass filled with ice and serve.

GLASS TYPE:
HIGHBALL

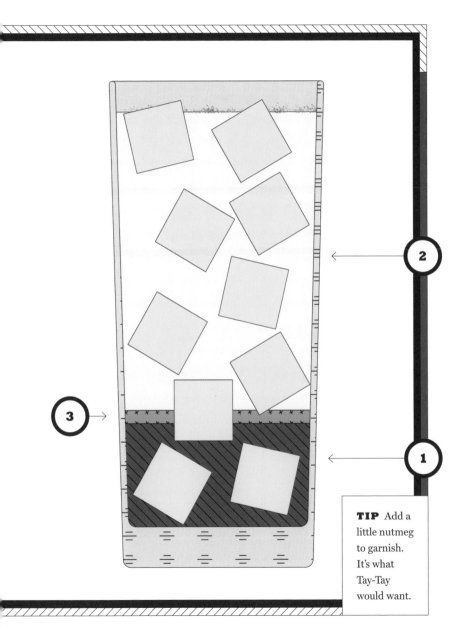

2

3

1

TIP Add a little nutmeg to garnish. It's what Tay-Tay would want.

MALTED BOURBON EGG CREAM

Your first egg cream always messes with your head: it contains neither egg nor cream, but it is just as creamy and frothy as if it did. The age-old American diner stalwart is a holy triad of sparkling water, milk and syrup, brought together by an essential (but very easy) technique. This lightly spiked version is deliciously yet mildly sweet, refreshing and moreish – you'll drink it in seconds. One note of caution: make sure the milk and seltzer are super chilled (a little time in the freezer is a great idea).

INGREDIENTS

1	bourbon	15 ml (½ oz)
2	full-fat (whole) dairy milk, extremely well chilled	120 ml (4 oz)
3	sparkling water, extremely well chilled	240 ml (8 oz)
4	malted syrup	3 tablespoons
5	vanilla extract	2–3 drops

EQUIPMENT Stirring spoon

METHOD Add all the ingredients to a highball with ice and stir vigorously with a long spoon until a thick froth appears on the surface. Serve immediately.

GLASS TYPE:
HIGHBALL

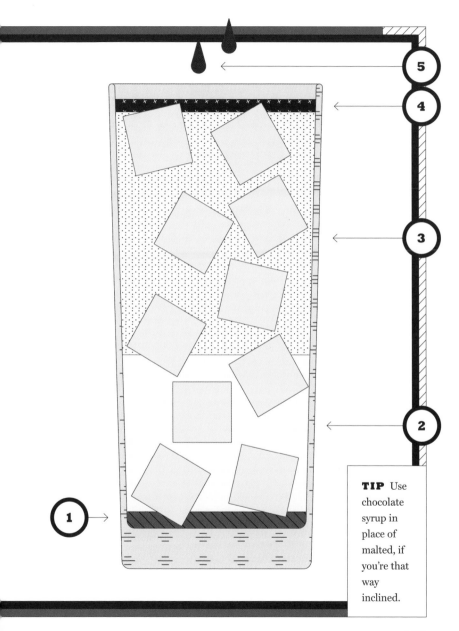

1

2

3

4

5

TIP Use chocolate syrup in place of malted, if you're that way inclined.

WHISKY & DRY

This classic of British pubs is the refreshing, wintertime drink when a tepid pint of bitter just won't do. 'Dry' refers to Canada Dry, the iconic ginger-soda mixer, often found gathering dust on the back bar, but almost any ginger ale will do. Make it posh with a slice of fresh ginger and lime. Best served with classic British snack food Twiglets with a Scampi Fries chaser (look it up).

INGREDIENTS

1	whisky	60 ml (2 oz)
2	lime juice, freshly squeezed	dash
3	ginger cordial	dash (optional)
4	ginger ale, chilled	80–100 ml (3–3½ oz)
5	lime wedge	to garnish
6	unpeeled fresh ginger, finger-sized slice	to garnish

EQUIPMENT British accent, i.e. 'there you go, babes'

METHOD Add the whisky and lime juice to a tumbler over ice. Add the cordial, if using, top with chilled ginger ale, add the lime wedge and fresh ginger to garnish.

GLASS TYPE:
TUMBLER

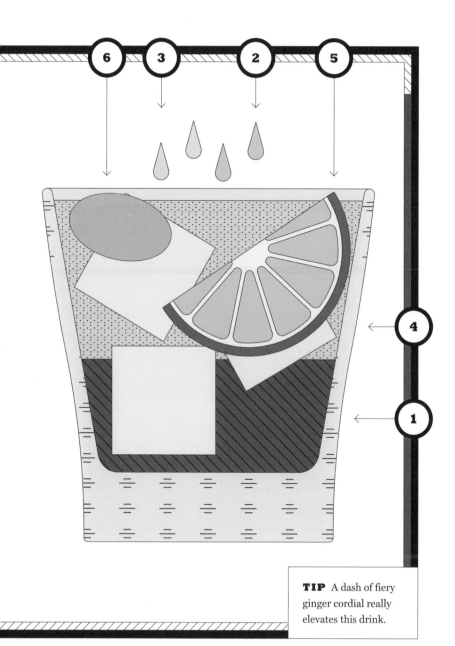

TIP A dash of fiery ginger cordial really elevates this drink.

EGG NOG

In the weeks before the festive holidays, when twinkling pop deity Mariah
Carey defrosts 'All I Want for Christmas Is You', there is but one drink to hold
in our mittened hands: eggnog. The chilled crème anglaise-like drink straddles
the line between delicious and weird, with its egg-heavy recipe and sweet,
melted ice-cream consistency. Whisky or bourbon gently spikes this dessert-
like cocktail, making it as intoxicating as the great Carey herself. Swap out the
vanilla seeds for a tablespoon of vanilla extract and the spiced syrup for simple
syrup, if need be. Keep chilled for one day ahead of serving.

INGREDIENTS (SERVE 6)

1	egg yolks	4 large
2	Big Cardamomma's House Syrup (page 40)	100 ml (3½ oz)
3	double (heavy) cream	100 ml (3½ oz)
4	full-fat (whole) milk	500 ml (17 oz)
5	whisky or bourbon	100–150 ml (3½–5 oz)
6	vanilla bean (pod), split, with seeds scraped out	1
7	cinnamon	pinch, to garnish

EQUIPMENT Blender, strainer

METHOD Add the egg yolks and syrup
to a blender and whizz for 2 minutes or until
pale. Add the cream, milk, whisky and vanilla
and blend again for a few seconds. Strain into
a glass over ice. Pinch of cinnamon to garnish.

GLASS TYPE:
TUMBLER

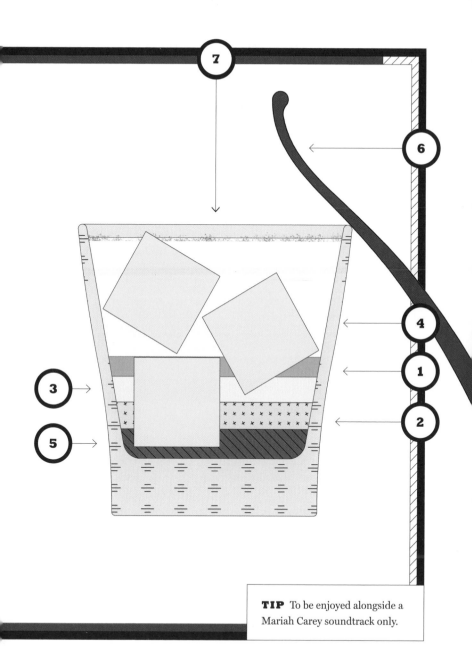

6

4

1

2

3

5

TIP To be enjoyed alongside a
Mariah Carey soundtrack only.

CRANBERRY SOUR

This all-weather, every-season drink really comes into its own in the later months. It's fresh, super dry and pleasantly opaque. You might also add a few fresh cranberries to the mix, but really, who has those lying around? A wedge of citrus will do perfectly.

INGREDIENTS

1	whisky	60 ml (2 oz)
2	cranberry juice, chilled	60 ml (2 oz)
3	orange juice, freshly squeezed, chilled	30 ml (1 oz)
4	lime juice, freshly squeezed	dash
5	Simple Syrup (page 38)	dash
6	ginger beer, chilled	60 ml (2 oz)
7	Angostura bitters	2–3 drops
8	pink grapefruit wedge	to garnish

EQUIPMENT Shaker

METHOD Shake the whisky, juices and syrup over ice. Strain into a glass, top with ginger beer and add bitters. Garnish.

GLASS TYPE:
TUMBLER

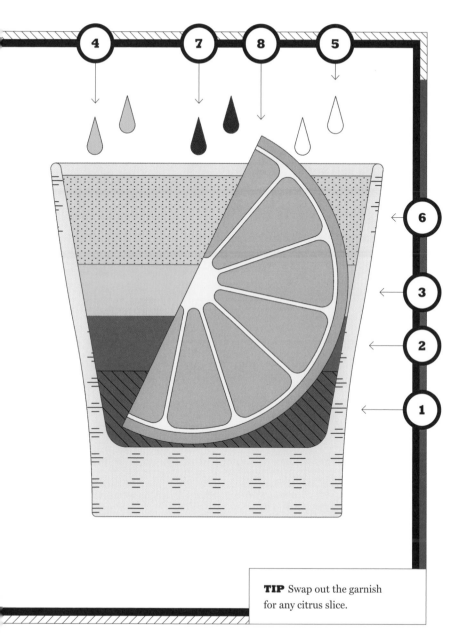

TIP Swap out the garnish for any citrus slice.

WASHINGTON APPLE

This elegant version of the dry, apple-edged, American-college cocktail uses pale gold Calvados apple brandy in place of sour apple schnapps (the latter, depending on which brand you reach for, seems to be mostly nuclear-bright red or green food dye). The natural ruby tone of the cranberry juice should do the trick.

INGREDIENTS

1	whisky	30 ml (1 oz)
2	cranberry juice	30 ml (1 oz)
3	Calvados apple brandy	30 ml (1 oz)
4	sliced red apple	to garnish

EQUIPMENT Shaker

METHOD Shake the liquids over ice until frosty. Pour into a glass and serve with apple slice as garnish.

GLASS TYPE:
COUPE

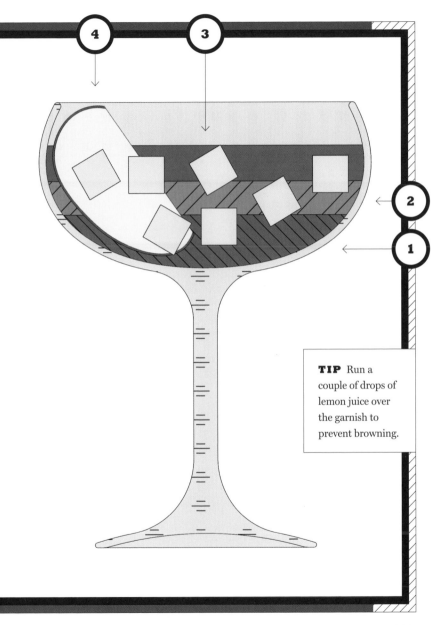

TIP Run a couple of drops of lemon juice over the garnish to prevent browning.

IRISH COFFEE

This classic dessert drink long graced the menus of homely 1980s steak restaurants; one of these and your dad's volume goes up to 11. The Irish Coffee is the whiskey-powered after-dinner pick-me-up that was insanely popular in olden times, when the Espresso Martini was a mere twinkle in a bartender's eye. It's time to reclaim this retro drink, which is just as delicious and rabble-rousing as ever.

INGREDIENTS

1	Irish whiskey	60 ml (2 oz)
2	hot filter coffee	150 ml (5 oz)
3	dark muscovado sugar	1 tablespoon
4	pouring cream	about 50 ml (1¾ oz)

EQUIPMENT Spoon

METHOD Add the whiskey, coffee and sugar to the mug and stir until the sugar is dissolved. Add cream to taste.

GLASS TYPE:
GLASS MUG

TIP Whip the cream so it sits on top and slowly melts into the drink.

BOULEVARDIER

With fiery Scotch at its base, this wintry classic has a tough-ass, slightly savoury flavour and an eye-catching dark tone. Perfect for poker night, or for summoning spirits. Make in a batch to keep your guests just the right side of inebriated.

INGREDIENTS

1	Scotch whisky	45 ml (1½ oz)
2	sweet vermouth	25 ml (¾ oz)
3	Campari	25 ml (¾ oz)
4	orange twist	to garnish

EQUIPMENT Mixing glass, stirring spoon, strainer

METHOD Stir the liquids with ice until frosty, then strain into a tumbler with rock ice. Garnish with an orange twist.

GLASS TYPE:
TUMBLER

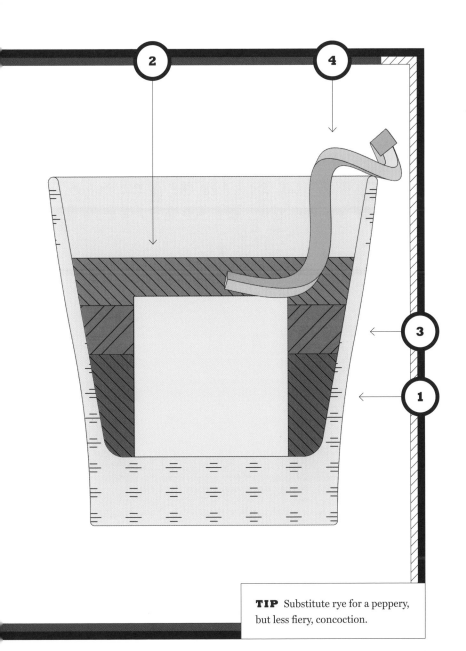

TIP Substitute rye for a peppery, but less fiery, concoction.

THE BEE STING

The Bee Sting has the healing powers of the Hot Toddy, only frosty – and with an elevated, floral honey edge. The sting comes in the form of fresh lemon juice that adds a sourness to make your hair curl. Used up all your homemade lavender honey syrup on your protein pancakes? Feel free to use a healthy glob of runny honey instead; it's just as delicious.

INGREDIENTS

1	bourbon	60 ml (2 oz)
2	honey lavender syrup	1 tablespoon
3	lemon juice, freshly squeezed	1 tablespoon
4	lemon wheel	to garnish

EQUIPMENT Shaker

METHOD Shake all the liquids vigorously with ice for 15 seconds. Strain into a glass over fresh ice and garnish with a lemon wheel.

GLASS TYPE:
TUMBLER

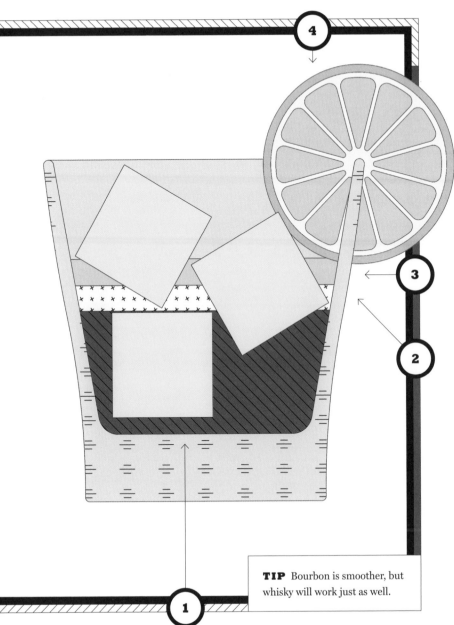

TIP Bourbon is smoother, but whisky will work just as well.

Mint Julep

This is the way to drink whisky: a little sugar, a lot of ice and a fresh injection of herbal mint. It's criminally simple to make, so elevate this delightful classic with metal cups or frozen highballs and invest in a set of metallic stirring straws. Worried about overdoing the mint garnish? Don't be. Each sprig should be tickling the drinker's nose.

INGREDIENTS

1	mint leaves	6–7
2	demerara sugar	1 teaspoon
3	bourbon	90 ml (3 oz)
4	sparkling water	splash (optional)
5	mint sprig	to garnish

EQUIPMENT Muddler

METHOD Add the mint leaves to your chilled cup or glass. Add sugar and squish lightly with a muddler. Add finely cracked ice, pour the bourbon over it and stir until the glass frosts. Top with more ice and stir again. Add sparkling water if using (just to take the edge off), garnish and serve.

GLASS TYPE:
TALL GLASS OR
METAL CUP

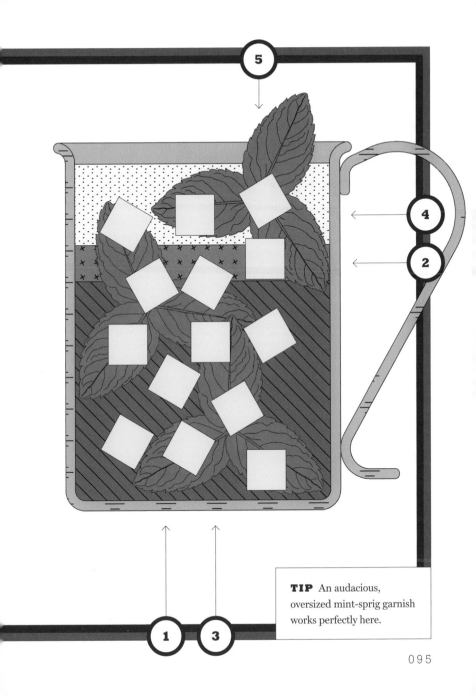

TIP An audacious, oversized mint-sprig garnish works perfectly here.

BOURBON FRENCH 75

Like countless other timeless cocktail recipes, the original French 75 – bright, tart and decadent – originated in Harry's New York Bar in Paris in 1915. This softer, brunch-ready version is just as refined, but swaps out gin and lemon for smooth bourbon, freshly squeezed orange juice and a little rosemary syrup for a subtle herbal tone. Top with Champagne or a simple dry prosecco.

INGREDIENTS

1	bourbon	30 ml (1 oz)
2	orange juice, freshly squeezed	30 ml (1 oz)
3	rosemary syrup (page 96)	15 ml (½ oz)
4	chilled Champagne	to top
5	orange twist	to garnish

EQUIPMENT Shaker

METHOD Shake the bourbon, juice and syrup over ice. Pour into a coupe or flute, top with chilled Champagne. Garnish with an orange twist and serve.

GLASS TYPE:
COUPE OR FLUTE

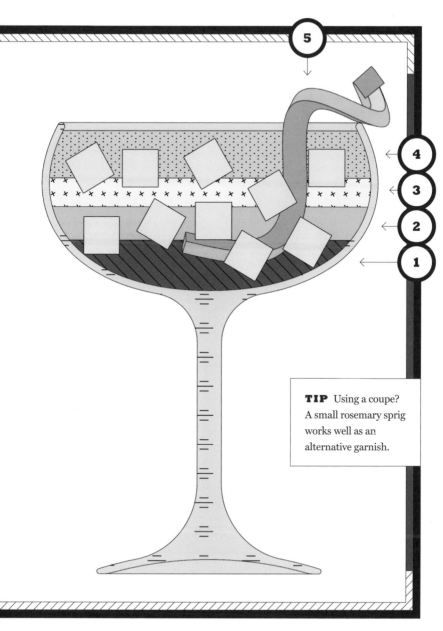

TIP Using a coupe? A small rosemary sprig works well as an alternative garnish.

NICE PEAR

Smooth bourbon and ripe pears are perfect bedfellows. The subtle sweetness of chilled pear juice turns up bourbon's natural vanilla and tobacco notes to create a masterful autumnal taste. A little lemon juice livens things up and keeps the sweetness in check.

INGREDIENTS

1	bourbon or rye	60 ml (2 oz)
2	pear juice	15 ml (½ oz)
3	lemon juice, freshly squeezed	dash
4	cardamom bitters	2–3 drops
5	pear slice	to garnish

EQUIPMENT Shaker

METHOD Shake the bourbon and juices over ice. Strain over ice into a tumbler, add bitters and garnish, then serve.

GLASS TYPE:
TUMBLER

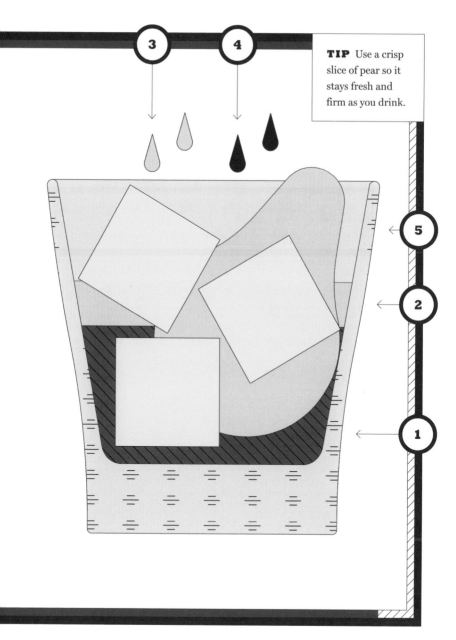

TIP Use a crisp slice of pear so it stays fresh and firm as you drink.

Spiced Mocha Hot Chocolate

This traditional mocha has an espresso and bourbon base, but with winter spices and a chilli kick. Feel free to be overly generous with the syrup but use just a little pinch of chilli to warm your cockles (or more to cure almost every illness known to man).

INGREDIENTS

1	bourbon	60 ml (2 oz)
2	plant-based milk	150 ml (5 oz)
3	organic cocoa (unsweetened chocolate) powder	1 tablespoon
4	Big Cardamomma's House Syrup (page 40)	1 tablespoon
5	espresso	shot
6	chilli powder	pinch

EQUIPMENT Milk pan or alternative small pan, wooden spoon

METHOD Heat the ingredients in a milk pan until hot but not boiling, stirring gently. Pour into a glass and serve.

GLASS TYPE:
THERMAL
GLASS OR MUG

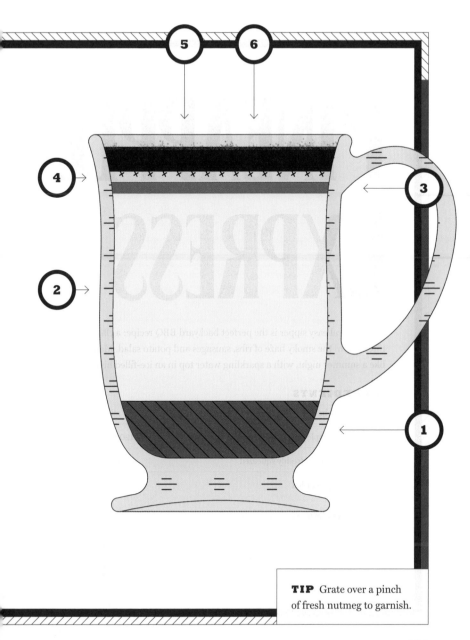

TIP Grate over a pinch
of fresh nutmeg to garnish.

PINEAPPLE EXPRESS

This tropical easy sipper is the perfect backyard BBQ recipe: a classy interlude in the smoky haze of ribs, sausages and potato salad. Make it long, like a summer night, with a sparkling water top in an ice-filled highball.

INGREDIENTS

1	bourbon	60 ml (2 oz)
2	pineapple juice, freshly squeezed, chilled	120 ml (4 oz)
3	lime juice, freshly squeezed	dash
4	ginger cordial	dash

EQUIPMENT Shaker, strainer

METHOD Shake the ingredients over ice. Strain and serve in a chilled coupe.

GLASS TYPE:
COUPE

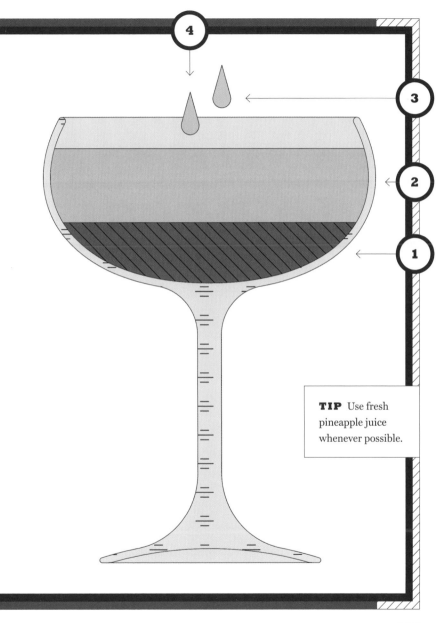

TIP Use fresh pineapple juice whenever possible.

PICKLE BACK

This party-starter/test of endurance will do one of two things: add a little theatre to get your night going, or completely derail your festivities 30 minutes after they've begun. Use a premium rye, bourbon or blended whisky (but not a fiery Scotch; you're not a monster). Chill your shot glasses for style.

INGREDIENTS

1	whisky	60 ml (2 oz)
2	brined pickle juice	60 ml (2 oz)
3	cornichon	to garnish
4	light beer	small, to chase

EQUIPMENT A little derring-do

METHOD Pour the whisky in one shot glass, the pickle brine into the other and add a cornichon on a cocktail stick balanced on top. Drink the whisky, then the brine, and finally, eat the cornichon. Serve with a small, icy-cold light beer as a chaser/mouth cleanser.

GLASS TYPE: SHOT
GLASSES OR TUMBLER

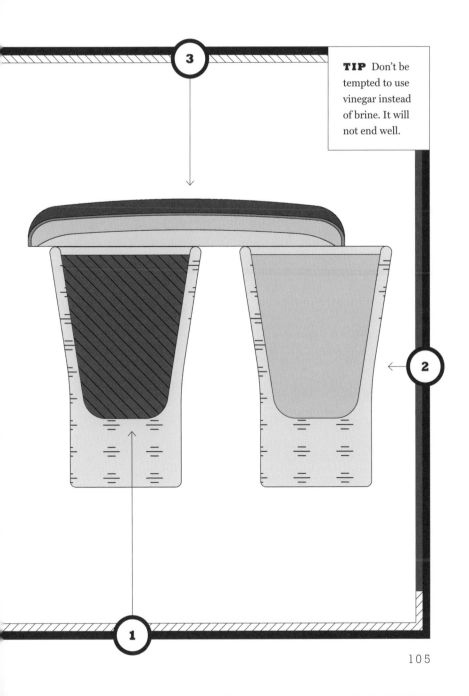

TIP Don't be tempted to use vinegar instead of brine. It will not end well.

THE BALL BOY

Inspired by summer tennis tournaments, this pink-toned thirst-quencher is as dry as the clay court at the French Open, and as lush as the Wimbledon lawns. Use a pre-made still lemonade, with little to no sugar. The perfect summer sipper.

INGREDIENTS

1	frozen honeydew melon balls	to garnish
2	bourbon	45 ml (1½ oz)
3	Chambord or premium raspberry liqueur	15 ml (½ oz)
4	fresh still lemonade	90 ml (3 oz)

EQUIPMENT Melon baller, a strong backhand

METHOD Fill a highball with 3–5 melon balls and crushed ice. Pour over the bourbon, Chambord and lemonade, and serve.

GLASS TYPE:
HIGHBALL

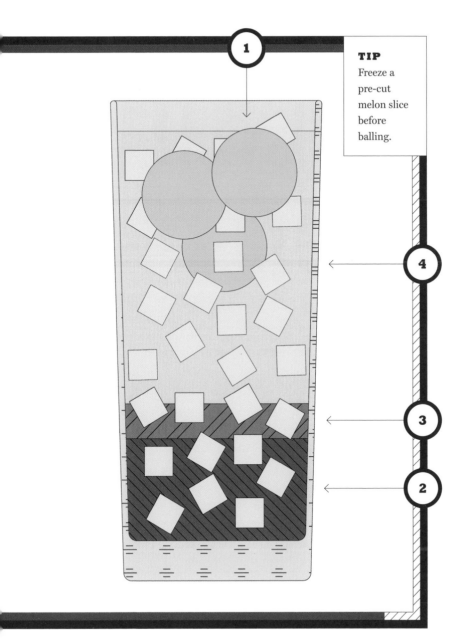

TIP
Freeze a pre-cut melon slice before balling.

MIDNIGHT IN THE PINES

Pine tips – the sweet, aromatic, and bright, new green needles at the end of fir twigs – make a delicious homemade syrup. Mix with bourbon and chilled, nutty almond milk, and you have yourself a delicious, sweet-smelling, forest-dwelling cocktail.

INGREDIENTS

1	bourbon	60 ml (2 oz)
2	almond milk, chilled	60 ml (2 oz)
3	Pine Tip Syrup (page 41)	15 ml (½ oz)
4	chocolate bitters	2–3 drops
5	pine tips	to garnish

EQUIPMENT Shaker

METHOD Shake the liquids (except the bitters and pine tips) over ice. Pour into a tumbler over ice, add bitters, then serve with freshly picked pine tips to garnish.

GLASS TYPE:
TUMBLER

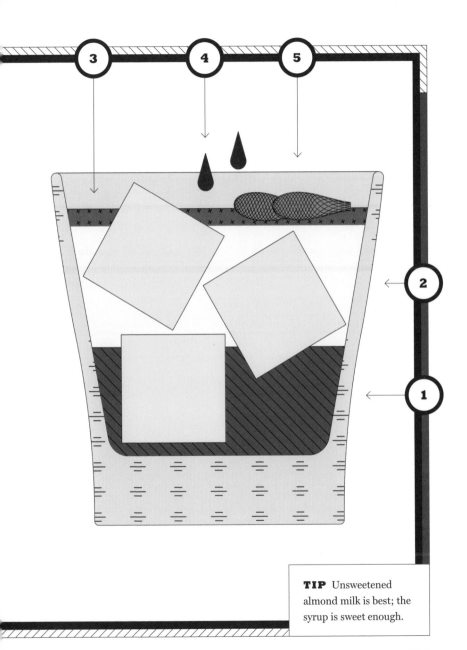

TIP Unsweetened almond milk is best; the syrup is sweet enough.

BERGAMOT TEA MARTINI

Temperature is essential for this one – the iciness will mellow out the whiskey and lift the bergamot-infused tea leaves to new heights. Keep it classy – otherwise, it's just a couple of shots of booze with a teabag thrown in. It's all in the mouth of the beholder.

INGREDIENTS

1	bourbon or rye	30 ml (1 oz)
2	vodka	30 ml (1 oz)
3	Earl Grey	1 teabag
4	dry vermouth	15 ml (½ oz)
5	orange bitters	2–3 drops
6	orange twist	to garnish

EQUIPMENT Shaker

METHOD Add the bourbon and vodka to a shaker, then add teabag and let steep for at least 30 minutes. Then remove the teabag, add the vermouth and shake over ice until frosty. Pour into a glass, then add the bitters and garnish.

GLASS TYPE:
COUPE

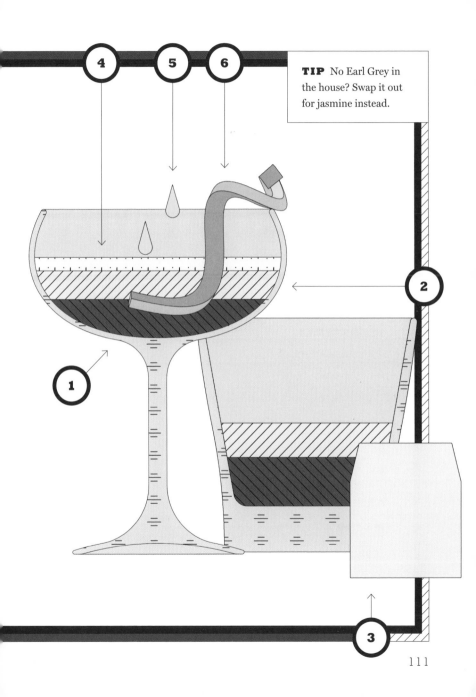

TIP No Earl Grey in the house? Swap it out for jasmine instead.

Ginger Greyhound

Refreshingly simple, an old-school Greyhound only has two main elements – booze and juice – but this whiskey version includes a little spicy syrup to add warmth and take the edge off, especially if your grapefruit juice is a little on the sour side.

INGREDIENTS

1	bourbon or rye	30 ml (1 oz)
2	pink grapefruit juice, freshly squeezed	100 ml (3½ oz)
3	Big Cardamomma's House Syrup (page 40)	dash
4	orange bitters	2–3 drops
5	lime twist	to garnish

EQUIPMENT Shaker

METHOD Shake the bourbon, juice and syrup over ice. Strain into a coupe and add bitters and garnish.

GLASS TYPE:
COUPE

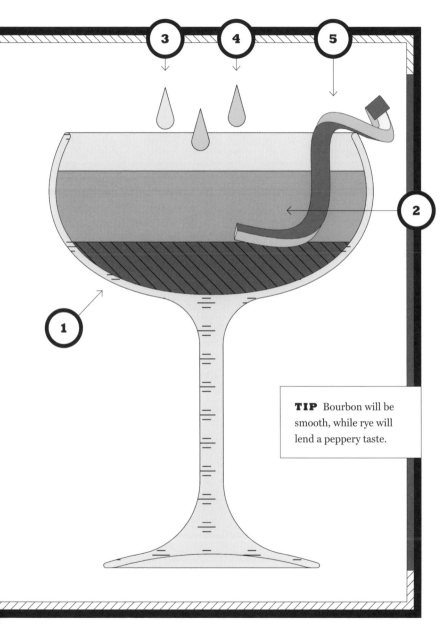

TIP Bourbon will be smooth, while rye will lend a peppery taste.

HONEY BEER PUNCH

A sweet, beery take on Long Island Iced Tea, with gin, honey and a premium brew creating a slip-down punch for one. Add more honey to taste.

INGREDIENTS

1	honey	1 teaspoon
2	hot water	splash
3	whisky	30 ml (1 oz)
4	lemon juice, freshly squeezed	15 ml (½ oz)
5	premium beer, chilled	80–100 ml (3–3½ oz)
6	lemon wheel	to garnish

EQUIPMENT Stirring spoon

METHOD Add the honey to the glass with a splash of hot water and stir with a spoon to loosen. Add ice, whisky and lemon juice and stir. Top with chilled beer and add garnish.

GLASS TYPE:
HIGHBALL

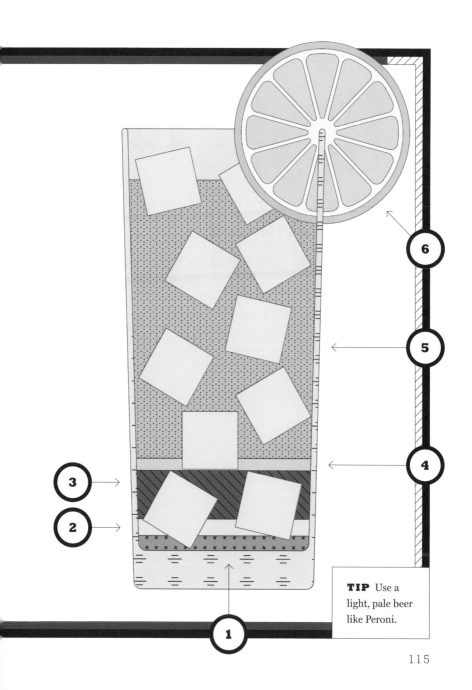

TIP Use a light, pale beer like Peroni.

STORMY & DARK

One of the finest ways to get tipsy is this whisky-powered version of the iconic Dark & Stormy. The original take on the refreshing and rather simple rum concoction is, unofficially, the national drink of Bermuda. This whisky version is just the ticket. Pour the whisky in first for a perfect mix – or add it in last and let it seep through the ice for a little drama.

INGREDIENTS

1	whisky	60 ml (2 oz)
2	lime juice, freshly squeezed	15 ml (½ oz)
3	chilled ginger beer	80–100 ml (3–3½ oz)
4	lime wheels	4, to garnish

EQUIPMENT Stirring spoon

METHOD Add the whisky and lime juice over ice and stir until frosty. Top with ginger beer and add garnish with lime wheels.

GLASS TYPE:
HIGHBALL

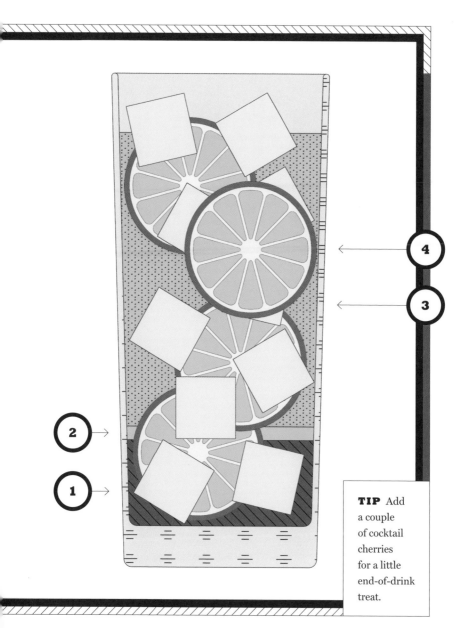

TIP Add a couple of cocktail cherries for a little end-of-drink treat.

DESERT PUNCH

The delicate, dark-peach colour of this citrus cocktail belies its smooth rye whiskey and chilli undertone. It has a rich, complex taste that's fresh and zingy, with a bright aroma and a tickle of desert heat.

INGREDIENTS

1	fresh chilli	sliver
2	rye	60 ml (2 oz)
3	lemon and orange juice mix, freshly squeezed	20 ml (⅔ oz)
4	Simple Syrup (page 38)	dash
5	orange bitters	2–3 drops
6	orange twist	to garnish

EQUIPMENT Mixing glass, muddler, strainer

METHOD Muddle the chilli in a mixing glass, add the rye, citrus juice, syrup, bitters and ice. Shake until super frosty. Strain into a chilled glass and garnish with an orange twist.

GLASS TYPE:
COUPE

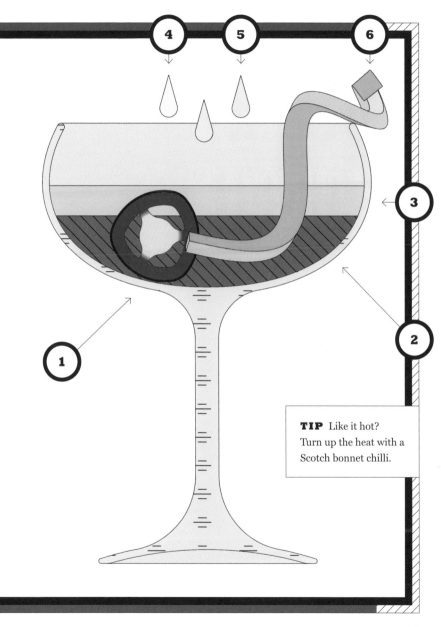

TIP Like it hot? Turn up the heat with a Scotch bonnet chilli.

GRANDMA'S HOUSE

The ingredients list of this bright, juicy cocktail may be a little like raiding your grandmother's booze cabinet (apricot brandy, Cointreau) but bear with it – it's a fresh, citrus, sherbet fizz of a drink that's multilayered (and rather strong).

INGREDIENTS

1	rye	60 ml (2 oz)
2	apricot brandy	15 ml (½ oz)
3	blood orange juice, freshly squeezed	120 ml (4 oz)
4	lemon juice, freshly squeezed	dash
5	Cointreau	15 ml (½ oz)
6	orange slice	to garnish
7	cocktail cherry	to garnish

EQUIPMENT Shaker

METHOD Shake the rye, apricot brandy and citrus juices over ice until frosty. Pour into ice-filled coupe. Drizzle Cointreau over the top, and add an orange slice and cherry to garnish.

GLASS TYPE:
COUPE

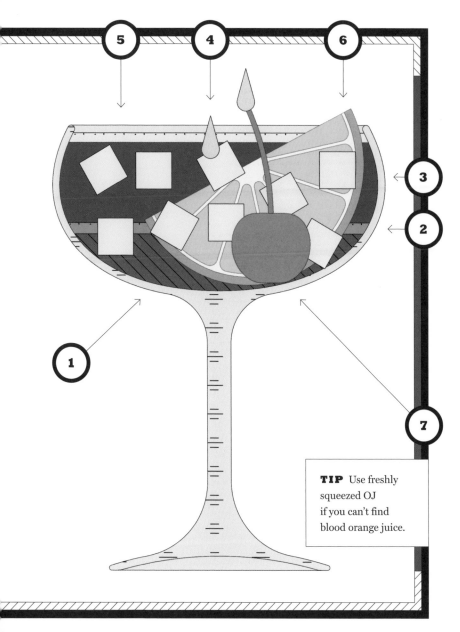

TIP Use freshly squeezed OJ if you can't find blood orange juice.

ROSE BUD

Lightly bitter grapefruit balanced with sweet and fragrant elderflower, underpinned with a power punch of light rum. A fragile-looking concoction that hides a real strength.

INGREDIENTS

1	rye	60 ml (2 oz)
2	St-Germain elderflower liqueur	30 ml (1 oz)
3	pink grapefruit juice, freshly squeezed	50 ml (1¾ oz)

EQUIPMENT Shaker

METHOD Add the liquids to a shaker. Shake over ice until frosty, then strain into a chilled coupe.

GLASS TYPE:
COUPE

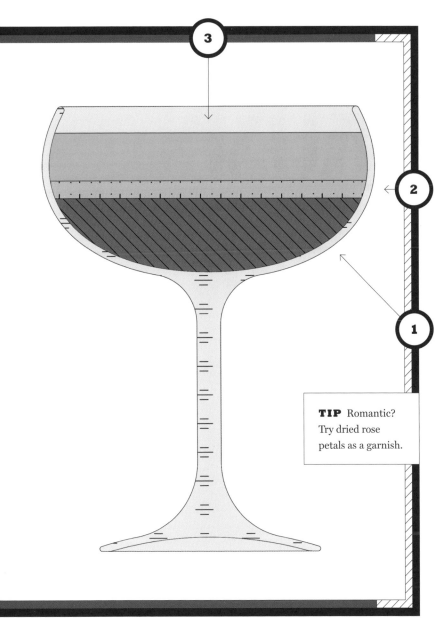

TIP Romantic? Try dried rose petals as a garnish.

BANANAS FOSTER 2.0

The iconic, retro, flambé banana dessert – popular in the 1980s – is reworked here as a frozen, blended whisky cocktail with added cinnamon. This recipe is foolproof, but requires the potential embarrassment of purchasing a bottle of banana liqueur (perhaps ask a friend to buy it on your behalf). Otherwise, it's delicious. A perfect dessert cocktail.

INGREDIENTS

1	whisky	60 (2 oz)
2	banana liqueur	25 ml (¾ oz)
3	banana, ripe	1 medium
4	premium vanilla ice cream	2 scoops
5	almond milk	dash (optional)
6	cinnamon	pinch, to garnish

EQUIPMENT Blender

METHOD Add the ingredients (except the almond milk and cinnamon) to a blender and whizz. Add the almond milk to loosen, if desired. Add the cinnamon. Serve in a highball.

GLASS TYPE:
HIGHBALL

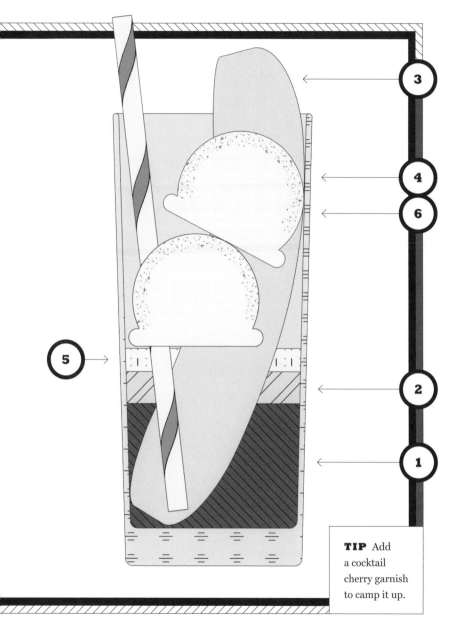

TIP Add a cocktail cherry garnish to camp it up.

GINGER OLD FASHIONED

There's a reason the Old Fashioned is considered one of the world's most iconic cocktails – it's perfectly balanced. Traditionally made with bourbon or rye whiskey, this ginger-powered version uses syrup from a stem ginger jar; it's sweet and fiery. Use a good-quality whiskey and don't omit the bitters: stay classy.

INGREDIENTS

1	stem ginger syrup	1 teaspoon
2	bourbon or rye	60 ml (2 oz)
3	Angostura bitters	2 drops
4	cocktail cherries	1–2, to garnish
5	large orange twist	to garnish

EQUIPMENT Stirring spoon

METHOD Add the syrup and bourbon to a tumbler with a large rock ice and stir. Add the bitters, cherries, flex the orange twist over the glass to release oils, add and serve.

GLASS TYPE:
TUMBLER

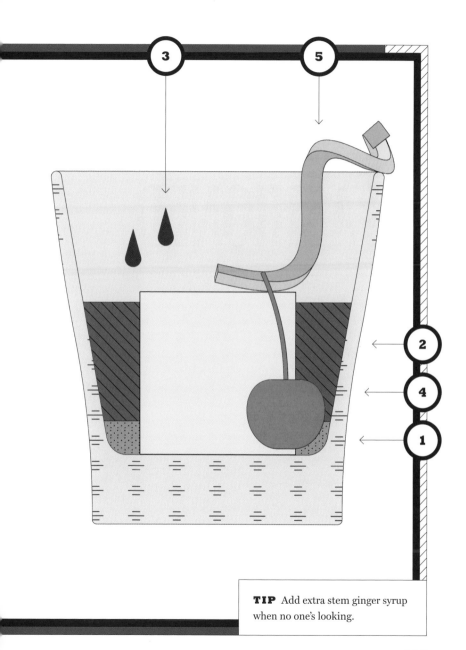

TIP Add extra stem ginger syrup when no one's looking.

HARD CIDER

Created for Americans who tend to forget to put alcohol in their cider, this delicious and smoky-sweet cloudy cocktail has a fresh, herby countryside taste and a mule's kick of smooth whiskey. Don't scrimp on the maple syrup and use the best (i.e. not the McDonald's pancake syrup you stockpile in your desk drawer).

INGREDIENTS

1	bourbon	60 ml (2 oz)
2	cloudy and tart apple juice	120 ml (4 oz)
3	maple syrup	10 ml (⅓ oz)
4	lemon juice, freshly squeezed	dash
5	thyme	2 small sprigs

EQUIPMENT Shaker

METHOD Shake the liquids and a sprig of thyme over ice until frosty. Pour into a coupe. Serve with remaining thyme sprig.

GLASS TYPE:
COUPE

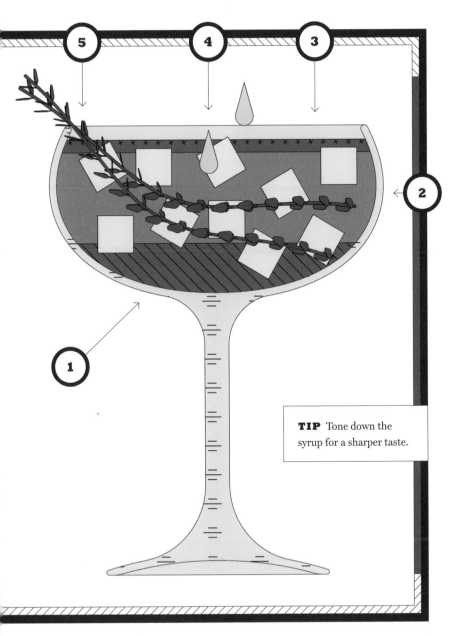

TIP Tone down the syrup for a sharper taste.

HOT SPICED GINGER PUNCH

Many of us consume at least eight pints too many of mulled wine each Christmas. This spiced pear, ginger and apple concoction is a perfect and rather fancy upgrade. Use the classiest apple juice you can find – either way, this will put festive hairs on your chest.

INGREDIENTS (SERVES 10)

1	whisky	250 ml (8½ oz)
2	Stone's Original Ginger Wine	250 ml (8½ oz)
3	cloudy apple juice	1.5 litres (52¾ oz)
4	mulled spice teabags	2
5	maple syrup	2 tablespoons
6	cinnamon sticks	2
7	crisp pears	2 slices

EQUIPMENT Milk pan or alternative small pan

METHOD Slowly warm the whisky, ginger wine, apple juice, teabags, syrup and cinnamon sticks to a very gentle, barely happening simmer for at least 10 minutes. Add pear slices to each glass, ladle the cocktail in and serve.

GLASS TYPE:
THERMAL
GLASS OR MUG

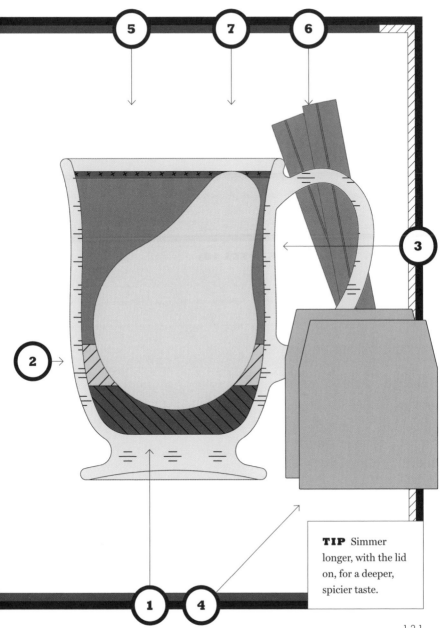

TIP Simmer longer, with the lid on, for a deeper, spicier taste.

NYC SOUR

Soft Pinot Noir and smoky bourbon, both tempered by a sharp shot of citrus. This unique Whiskey Sour, beloved in NYC, has two contrasting tones, making it pleasingly showy as well as surprisingly delicious. Just like New York City itself, it shouldn't work, but it does.

INGREDIENTS

1	bourbon	60 ml (2 oz)
2	Simple Syrup (page 38)	15 ml (½ oz)
3	lemon juice, freshly squeezed	30 ml (1 oz)
4	Pinot Noir or similar light red wine	30 ml (1 oz)
5	lemon twist	to garnish

EQUIPMENT Shaker, strainer

METHOD Shake the bourbon, syrup and lemon juice over ice until frosty. Pour into a tumbler with rock ice, and very slowly pour the wine over so it magically balances. Add a lemon twist to garnish.

GLASS TYPE:
TUMBLER

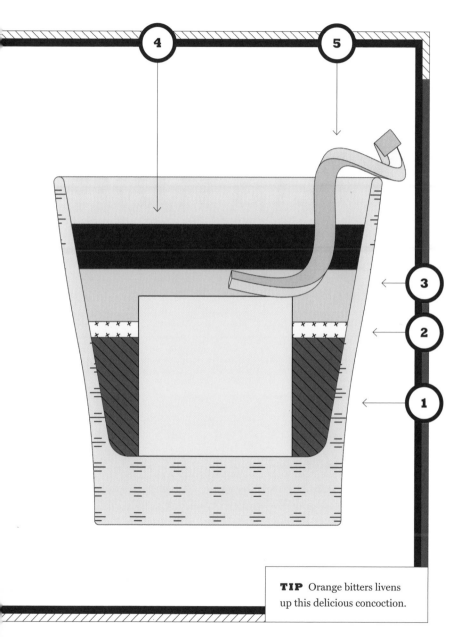

TIP Orange bitters livens up this delicious concoction.

Dark Ruby

Ruby red and delicious. The rosemary syrup, although not essential, underlines the Campari's herbal undertones. And the chilled prosecco makes it classy.

INGREDIENTS

1	whisky	25 ml (¾ oz)
2	Campari	25 ml (¾ oz)
3	lemon juice, freshly squeezed	1 tablespoon
4	rosemary syrup	1 tablespoon
5	dry prosecco	to top
6	lime twist	to garnish

EQUIPMENT Shaker, strainer

METHOD Shake the whisky, Campari, lemon juice and syrup over ice until frosty. Strain into a chilled coupe, and top with prosecco. Add lime twist to garnish.

GLASS TYPE:
COUPE

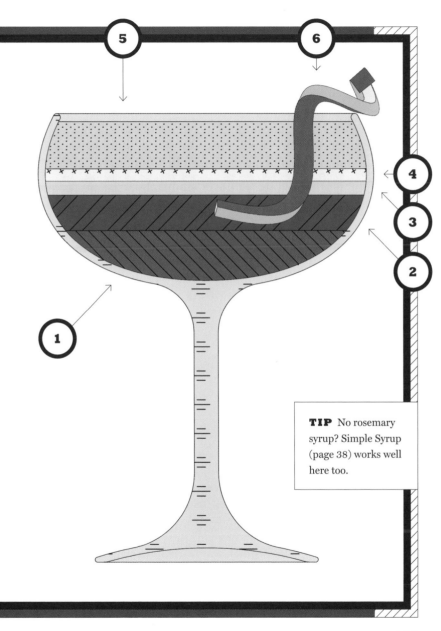

TIP No rosemary syrup? Simple Syrup (page 38) works well here too.

SPIKED CHERRY COLA

If being an adult is insanely boring, there is one thing that makes it sweeter: doing everything you did as a kid, but with alcohol. Behold, the Spiked Cherry Cola with whisky or bourbon, cherry liqueur, cola and a little lemon juice to temper the sweetness. Being a kid was never this good.

INGREDIENTS

1	whisky	60 ml (2 oz)
2	Cherry Heering liqueur	20 ml (⅔ oz)
3	lemon juice, freshly squeezed	dash
4	organic cola	to top
5	cocktail cherries	2, to garnish
6	lime twist	to garnish

EQUIPMENT Stirring spoon

METHOD Add whisky, cherry liqueur and lemon juice to a highball with ice and stir. Pour cola on top, and add cherries and the lime twist to garnish.

GLASS TYPE:
HIGHBALL

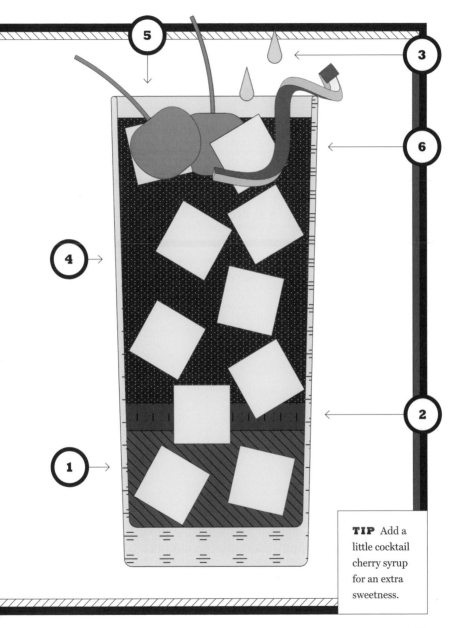

TIP Add a little cocktail cherry syrup for an extra sweetness.

Man O' War

This Manhattan meets Whiskey Sour cocktail is thought to have been inspired by the Man O' War himself, the early to mid-1900s American Thoroughbred horse with countless wins under his, um, saddle; it simply must be tried. Although the question remains: yay or neigh?

INGREDIENTS

1	bourbon	60 ml (2 oz)
2	Grand Marnier or triple sec	30 ml (1 oz)
3	lemon juice, freshly squeezed	15 ml (½ oz)
4	sweet vermouth	15 ml (½ oz)
5	orange twist	to garnish

EQUIPMENT Shaker, strainer

METHOD Shake the bourbon, Grand Marnier, lemon juice and vermouth over ice until frosty. Strain into a chilled coupe. Garnish with the orange twist.

GLASS TYPE:
COUPE

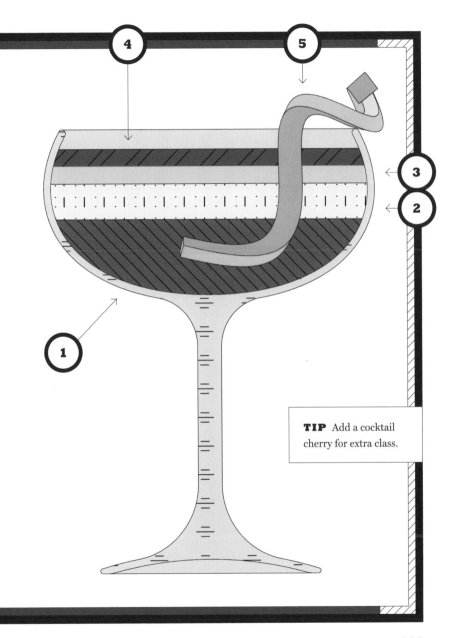

TIP Add a cocktail cherry for extra class.

INDEX

ABOUT DAN JONES

Perhaps the world's most prolific cocktail enjoyer and best-selling author of *Gin: Shake, Muddle, Stir* and *Rum: Shake, Muddle, Stir*, Dan Jones is a British writer and editor. A self-professed homebody, he is well versed in the art of at-home drinking and loves to entertain, constantly researching his cocktail craft and trying out new recipes.